Editor: David Barlex

Teacher's Guide
Authors: David Barlex with Jo Compton

Capability Task File
Authors: David Barlex, Eileen Barlex
Illustrations: Nathan Barlex and Jo Compton

Addison Wesley Longman Limited
Edinburgh Gate, Harlow, Essex, CM20 2JE
© The Nuffield Foundation 1996

All rights reserved. No part of this publication (with the exception of the
Capability Tasks on pages 45–92) may be reproduced,
stored in a retrieval system, or transmitted in any form or by any means,
electronic, mechanical, photocopying, recording,
or otherwise, without either the prior written permission of the Publishers
or a license permitting restricted copying issued by the Copyright Agency Ltd,
90 Tottenham Court Road, London, W1P 9HE.

First published in 1996
Second impression 1997
ISBN 0 582 29070 8

Design by Linda Males
Printed in Great Britain
by Pindar plc
Set in Minion 12/15pt

The Publishers' policy is to use paper manufactured from sustainable forests.

Contents

Part 1 Teaching D&T to 14–16 year-olds

Page

1	Introduction	1
2	Learning activities	2
3	Using Resource Tasks	3
4	Using the Student's Book	7
5	Using Capability Tasks	16
6	Assessment	23
7	Different Examination Boards	31
8	Resource Task Summary Tables	38

Part 2 Capability Tasks for 14–16 year-olds

	Capability Task Summary Tables	42

Fashion accessories

1	Home comforts	45
2	Themed scarves	48

Bags and carriers

3	Customized carriers	52
4	Feely bags unlimited	55

Interiors

5	Character hotels	58
6	Squashy seats	62

Kites

7	Kite bonanza	65

Protection

8	Clean cuisine	68
9	Travel safe	72

Street style

10	Happy cotton	75
11	Rap wrap	79

Tents

12	Snuggly buggly	82

The theatre

13	A cast of thousands	85
14	Audition kit bag	89

Part 1

Teaching D&T to 14–16 year-olds

Introduction 1

The Nuffield approach to design and technology has already proved extremely successful. At the time of writing it is being used by over one-third of the secondary schools in England and Wales. It is quite clear that the Nuffield Project's slogan 'Teaching students to design what they are going to make and then make what they have designed' is no idle boast. These materials have been designed to build on this proven approach but it is important to note that a school can use the materials 'from scratch' with students who have not met the approach previously. By using the approach and the associated materials, schools will be able to meet the requirements of the 1995 Statutory Orders for design and technology and prepare students for a variety of different examination board syllabuses. Quite deliberately the Nuffield approach is not allied to any one examination board but the Nuffield Project has worked closely with a number of different examination boards and this *Guide* describes how the materials can be used to meet different examination boards' requirements.

This *Teacher's Guide* deals with the focus area of design and technology most commonly called 'Textiles'. The publications for this area are shown below.

Textiles Student's Book

A complete text book to support the pupils in producing course work, learning the substance of design and technology, and tackling written examinations. You will need class sets with, ideally, each pupil having access to their own copy.

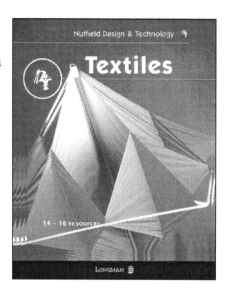

Textiles Resource Tasks File

This is a once-only purchase containing over 30 focused practical tasks as photocopy masters. Through these tasks you can teach the content required for GCSE success.

Textiles Teacher's Guide

This is a once-only purchase. Part 1 explains how to use the published materials and how to construct a scheme of work suitable for your school and examination board. Part 2 contains 14 different Capability Tasks.

2 Learning activities

If you teach design and technology the Nuffield way then you will use three different teaching methods.

- **Resource Tasks** These are short practical activities. They have been designed to make students think and to help them acquire the knowledge and skill they need to design and make really well.

- **Case Studies** These are true stories about design and technology in the world outside school. By reading them students find out more than they possibly could through designing and making alone. Through Case Studies they will learn about the way firms and businesses design and manufacture goods and how those goods are marketed and sold. They will also learn about the impact that products have on the people who use them and the places where they are made.

- **Capability Tasks** These involve designing and making a product that works. Students use what they have learned in Resource Tasks and Case Studies when they tackle a Capability Task. Capability Tasks take a lot longer than either Resource Tasks or Case Studies. You will need to organize your lessons so that students do the Resource Tasks and Case Studies they need for a Capability Task as part of the Capability Task. In this way you can make sure that your students can be successful in their designing and making.

The way these methods work together is shown here in this extract from the *Student's Book*.

Using Resource Tasks 3

A new design for 14–16 year-olds

Each Resource Task is presented to the student as an instruction sheet laid out like this.

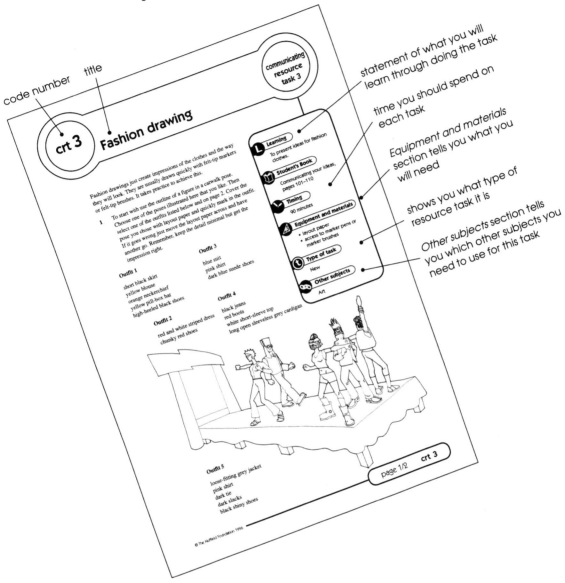

The design is different from that used earlier while still incorporating its key features and it has two additional features appropriate for 14–16 year-olds. These are an indication of the type of task (see page 4) and the links with other subjects.

You may organize the lesson so that everyone is doing the same Resource Task, set different students different tasks or allow them to choose from a range of Resource Tasks. Sometimes the tasks require students to work on their own and sometimes as part of a team.

Chapters 4–11 of the *Textiles Student's Book* contain cross-references to Resource Tasks, as shown below, indicating that the information on this page will be useful in tackling that particular Resource Task.

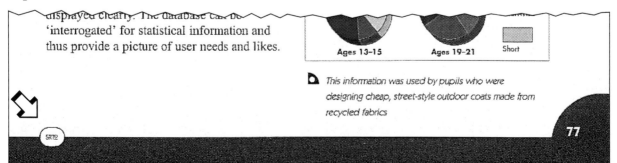

③ Types of Resource Task

There are three basic types of Resource Task.

- **Recapitulation Resource Tasks** These are tasks that go over things that students have probably done earlier. They are very useful for reminding students of things they may have forgotten or for catching up on things they have missed.

- **Extension Resource Tasks** These are tasks that take an idea that students were probably taught earlier and develop it further. They are useful for both revising earlier ideas and helping students use them in a more advanced way.

- **New ideas Resource Tasks** These are tasks that deal with knowledge and understanding that are new to 14–16 year-olds. It is unlikely that students will have done this sort of work earlier. They are important for helping students make progress.

You can use these classifications in a number of ways. You can organize sequences of Resource Tasks in a way that shows students the progress they can make by working through the sequence. Students who are facing difficulties can spend longer on recapitulation tasks. Particularly able students can miss out recapitulation tasks altogether.

Style and range of learning through Resource Tasks

The style of learning is *active*. It always involves a response from the student. Students might have to explain, record, design, construct, investigate or test. The learning intentions for any one Resource Task are likely to be quite narrow, but where possible tasks have been written that meet several learning intentions. In this way Resource Tasks can be used very efficiently.

Substance of Resource Tasks

The Resource Tasks are divided into eight sets as shown in Table 1. Four of these sets are developments of earlier Resource Tasks and there are four new sets for 14–16 year-olds – 'Decorative techniques', 'Fabric construction', 'Manufacturing' and 'Lines of interest'.

Through the Decorative techniques tasks students will become familiar with tie-dyeing and batik. Through the fabric construction tasks students will learn how to construct fabrics by knitting and layering, become familiar with different fabric constructions and understand their effect on physical properties. The Manufacturing task will enable students to learn how to operate batch production systems for a textile product and achieve quality assurance. The Lines of interest tasks will help students to learn a wide range of practical skills particularly suited to the designing and making of certain textile products. Where possible these tasks include an introduction to a fabric decoration technique or a fabric construction technique. You can find a detailed summary of all the textile Resource Tasks on pages 38–40.

Table 1 – Textiles Resource Tasks

Strategies	Communicating	Decorative techniques
SRT 1 Identifying needs and likes	CRT 1 Mood boards and theme boards	DRT 1 Tie-and-dye with natural dyes
SRT 2 Questionnaires	CRT 2 Presenting data	DRT 2 Batik snowflakes
SRT 3 Design briefs and specifications	CRT 3 Fashion drawing	
SRT 4 Brainstorming	CRT 4 Capturing fabric on paper	
SRT 5 Attribute analysis	CRT 5 Exploring interiors	
SRT 6 Evaluating	CRT 6 Communicating to the maker	
SRT 7 Systems and control		

Fabric construction	Manufacturing	Lines of interest
FCRT 1 Layering	MfRT 1 Rally arm bands	LIRT 1 Fashion accessories
FCRT 2 Knitting		LIRT 2 Bags and carriers
FCRT 3 Fabric construction investigation		LIRT 3 Interiors
		LIRT 4 Kites
		LIRT 5 Protection
		LIRT 6 Street style
		LIRT 7 Tents
		LIRT 8 The theatre

Health and safety	Products and applications	
HSRT 1 Health and safety	PART 1 Investigating a single product	
	PART 2 Investigating a collection of products	

Using Resource Tasks

3 Organizing the classroom

Following these guidelines will help ensure that Resource Task work is effective.

- Each student should have a copy of the instruction sheets.

- Each student should have a separate copy of any tables or worksheets required to be filled in during the task. Make sure that some spares are available for mistakes.

- Allow sufficient time and if necessary deviate from the recommended time.

- Ensure that the required materials, tools and equipment are readily available.

- Use a circus approach within your classroom to avoid equipment shortfalls.

- If necessary, go through the task with the class beforehand so that all students have clear targets for doing and recording.

- If necessary, demonstrate skills that will be needed in the task.

- If you require the students to tackle a sequence of Resource Tasks over successive lessons, share this with the class.

- Once the students are tackling the task, support them by asking questions, giving assistance, looking at what they write and draw, helping with practical difficulties and providing encouragement.

A teacher sets up a sequence of Resource Tasks over successive lessons and goes through the first task

Using the Student's Book 4

The *Student's Book* provides support for all aspects of GCSE courses. All Student's Books have the same overall structure, ensuring continuity of treatment whatever the focus area. The purpose and key features of each section of the Textiles Student's Book are described below.

Chapter 1 Doing Nuffield D&T for 14–16 year-olds

This chapter is divided into three parts.

Part 1 Learning D&T

This gives a clear description of the sorts of products that students will design and make and an explanation of the Nuffield approach. The use of Resource Tasks, Capability Tasks and Case Studies is described and there is guidance on reviewing progress during a Capability Task, evaluating the final product and assessing overall progress.

Part 2 Using other subjects in D&T

This identifies ways students can use art, science, mathematics and information technology to enhance designing and making.

Part 3 How you will be assessed at GCSE

This gives guidance on how to develop and carry out a Capability Task for GCSE course work and how to research and write a Case Study for GCSE course work. It also describes four types of questions used for GCSE written, terminal examinations.

You can use this part of the *Student's Book* as the basis for whole-class teaching about the way students will learn and as a basis for helping individual students with particular difficulties. For example, you might ask a student to read the section on using science and identify some science that he/she has been taught earlier if they are tackling a Capability Task in which science is likely to be useful. This could become the basis for the student talking to both their science and D&T teachers about ways in which the science could be applied.

Chapter 2 Examination questions

A range of examination questions, approved by SCAA, and typical of those likely to be set for GCSE written, terminal examinations is presented with comments.

Chapter 3 Case Studies

There are two sorts of Case Studies. Firstly, a set that is common to all the Student's Books whatever the focus area. These deal with the technologies which really affect the way people live. Often they are associated with a particular time in history. Reading these will help students understand the way that technology affects our lives. Secondly, there are those that deal with products that are similar to those that the students will be designing and making. They will describe the following about these products:

- how the designs were developed, manufactured, marketed and sold
- how the products work
- how the products affect people – those who make them, those who use them and others.

A particular study may deal with just one of these or the study may describe all of them. Through reading these studies students will gain an insight into professional practice which will inform their own designing and making.

There are two devices to help students read the studies. First, 'Pause for thought' boxes that ask intriguing questions but do not require the reader to write anything down. They are there to provide motivation to read more. Second, 'Questions' boxes. You can use these as staging posts for reading a Case Study as a class activity. For example, you could instruct the class as follows: 'I want you to spend 15 minutes reading this Case Study and discussing the questions with your partner. Then I want you to answer the questions in writing. This should take you a further 10 minutes.' The Case Studies also contain research activities. You can set these for homework as they involve finding out information that is not in the Case Study.

The titles of the Case Studies are shown in Table 2 below.

You can find a summary of their links to Capability Tasks in the Capability Task Summary Tables on pages 42–44.

Table 2 – Textiles Case Studies

General case studies	Focused case studies
Designing our surroundings	A textile designer's story
Technological endeavours	Bags and carriers
Information – the power to change lives	Corporate clothing
DIY medical testing	Design in the High Street
Manufacturing aircraft	New fashion textiles
Public transport in London	A tent for your home
	Protective clothing
	Saidpur women textile group Bangladesh
	Energy to make things work
	Colour and colourways
	Clothing manufacture
	Textile time line

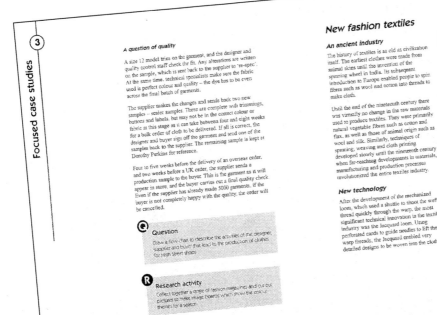

Chapter 4 Strategies for designing

This chapter revisits and develops strategies that may have been learned previously and introduces some new strategies for 14–16 year-olds. The strategies are shown in Table 3 below. The aim of this chapter is to provide the student with a repertoire of strategies and sufficient understanding to be able to choose and use them appropriately.

Table 3 – Strategies for 14–16 year-olds

Strategy	Strategy
Identifying needs and likes	Using computers
PIES	Applying science
observing people	checking on material choice
asking questions	stretchiness
using books and magazines	necessary investigations
image boards	Systems thinking
questionnaires	systems and subsystems
Design briefs	input, output and feedback
Specifying the product	systems boundaries
Generating design ideas	Automation
brainstorming	Planning
attribute analysis	Gannt charts
observational drawing	flow charts
investigative drawing	Evaluating
Modelling	user trip
thumbnail sketches	winners and losers
cut-outs	performance testing
annotated drawings	appropriateness
toiles	
swatch collections	

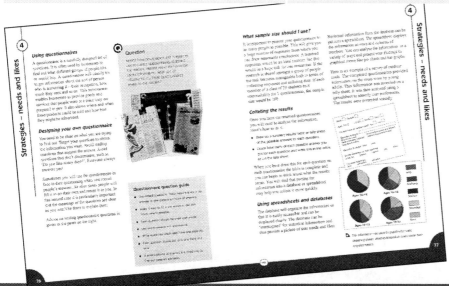

Note: A new video, 'Talent & Technology', featuring good examples of CAD and quick response manufacturing in the textiles industry, is available from Smith & Smith, 93 Sumatra, London NW6 1PT, for £19.99, inc. p&p. Tel: 0171 435 3749

Chapter 5 Communicating design proposals

This chapter builds on the Nuffield approach in detailing the techniques used by designers to communicate with clients, manufacturers and users. The aim of this chapter is to enable the student to choose and use techniques that are appropriate for the information to be conveyed. Table 4 below summarizes the techniques and purposes dealt with in this chapter.

Table 4 – Communication techniques for 14–16 year-olds

What you want to communicate	Techniques to use
choice of colours	mood boards
marketing information	line graphs
	bar charts
	pie charts
	theme boards
impression of clothes being worn	fashion drawing
detailed appearance of textile items	rendered drawings plus swatches
interior design	plans
	elevations
	perspective views
how to make an item	patterns
how to use/care for an item	printed information

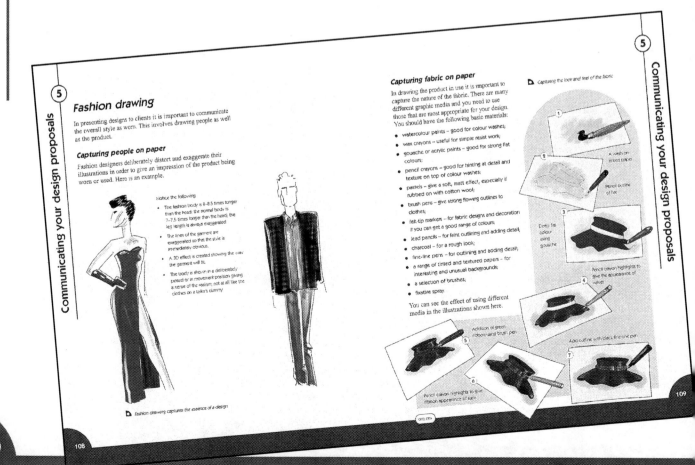

Chapter 6 Design Guides

The Nuffield Project has developed the idea of a line of interest as a means of limiting the sort of product that students in a class might design and make. This makes the teaching of a Capability Task much more manageable. A line of interest describes a particular type of product and the Nuffield Project has suggested the following eight lines of interest suitable for Textiles:

- Fashion accessories
- Bags and carriers
- Interiors
- Kites
- Protection
- Street style
- Tents
- Theatre.

Chapter 6 contains a design guide for each of these lines of interest. Each of these guides deals with the issues that should be considered when designing within this line of interest. They set an agenda for the students rather than providing the answers. The design guides provide a straightforward way for students to become familiar with areas of textile design. They can act as a stimulus for students who are having difficulty in deciding on their main course work. They can provide a reminder during a Capability Task to ensure that important issues are not overlooked. You can use the design guides in a number of ways.

- In one-to-one conversations with individual students as in 'I'm not sure that you've thought about all the important things here; let's look at the design guide to see if you've missed anything'.

- In conversations with small groups as in 'I want you to use the design guide to find four questions to ask each other about your design ideas. I'll be back in ten minutes to see how you're getting on'.

- In a question-answer session with the whole class as in 'It says here that there are lots of different influences on street style. Jane, I want you to use the example of 'Teddy Boys' and explain what this means. Then Paul I want you to give me another example where a recent fashion from the past is influencing street style now'.

- As a reading homework in preparation for a Capability Task which you can build on with a question-and-answer session the following lesson.

There is a final section in this chapter which deals with designing for fit. It describes the measurements required in order to use a ready-bought pattern for good fit and how such patterns might be adapted through adding or subtracting design details.

Chapter 7 Surface decoration techniques

This chapter describes the following decoration techniques by means of sequences of illustrations:

- dyeing using Dylon cold water dye
- tie-dyeing
- batik
- direct painting
- spray painting
- transfer printing
- block printing
- screen printing
- appliqué
- quilting
- hand embroidery
- free machine embroidery.

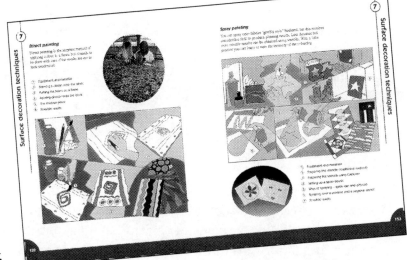

Clearly the information will not impart the tacit know-how required to use these techniques safely and effectively. As with making skills, there is no substitute for clear skill instruction and the opportunity to practise, so it is important that you use sound demonstration linked to appropriate Resource Tasks to enable students to develop their surface decoration skills.

Chapter 8 Fibres and yarns

The aim of this chapter is to provide students with an overview of fibre properties and yarn production. It builds on previous work by presenting a more extensive treatment of the sources of fibres and a description of the industrial production of both natural and synthetic yarns. It describes the performance of fibres in terms of the following qualities:

- cleanliness and washability
- absorbency
- effect of heat
- clothes moths
- bleaching
- strength
- effect of light
- dyeing
- shrinkage
- resilience and elasticity
- mildew.

It explains how different fibres can be combined to produce fabrics of particular properties.

It describes how students can spin their own yarns and dye them with either natural or synthetic dyes.

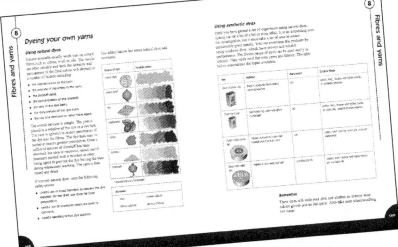

Chapter 9 Fabrics

This chapter provides students with an overview of fabric production methods and an understanding of the features which control fabric properties. The first part of this chapter describes the principles of knitting and weaving and how such operations are carried out industrially, with a clear indication of the level of

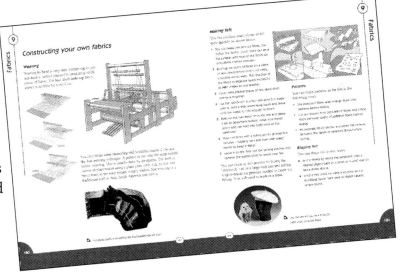

control technology needed for successful operation. It continues with a description of the industrial production, manipulation and uses of felt and a listing of other non-woven/non-knitted fabrics. Finally there is a description of commercial finishing processes.

The second part of the chapter describes the relationship between fabric properties, the constituent fibre(s) and the method of construction. It also describes how students can construct their own fabrics through hand knitting, machine knitting, weaving with a four-shaft loom, felt-making and layering.

Chapter 10 Information for textile product design

Choosing materials is a key part of design and technology. Information about materials is presented as a series of Chooser Charts. The aim of this chapter is to enable students to justify their materials choice.

Initially it presents two Chooser Charts describing fabric properties. The first chart describes named fabrics in terms of:

- weight
- strength
- inflammability
- drape
- resilience
- aftercare
- appearance
- absorbency
- cost.

The second chart lists fabrics in rank order according to their performance under these categories (with the exception of appearance).

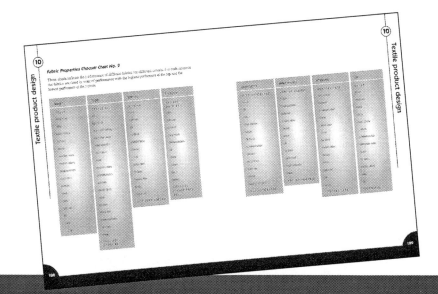

The third Chooser Chart describes a wide range of surface decoration techniques in terms of:

- one-off or repetitive
- time needed
- simple or complex.
- when to do it
- special equipment

The fourth Chooser Chart deals with the feel of fabrics and describes them in terms of:

- weight
- resilience
- texture.

The fifth Chooser Chart describes a wide range of fastenings in terms of:

- ease of use
- ease of fitting
- variety of types
- strength
- ease of care
- cost.

This is accompanied by an account of fastening conventions.

Chapter 11 Ways to make your product

The chapter starts by presenting a detailed overview of the making process under the following headings.

1. Making the overall plan of action
2. Buying the fabric, fastenings and consumable materials (sewing thread, embroidery thread, dyes, etc.)
3. Checking that necessary equipment is available
4. Dyeing or decorating fabric if required
5. Laying out the pattern on cheap fabric
6. Make up model sample, pressing and checking throughout
7. Checking for fit, shape, ease of wear, opinion of user(s)
8. Adjust pattern if needed and replan the order of construction, if needed
9. Press fabric
10. Lay out the pattern according to planned layout
11. Cut out the fabric
12. Make up the garment pressing and checking throughout
13. Final pressing
14. Check for fit, shape, drape, ease of wear, opinion of user(s), etc. and make any final minor adjustments

It takes as an example the making of a striped baby grow.

The chapter then provides an overview of the way the overall shape and fit of any textile item is governed by three features:

- the shapes of the pieces of fabric as they are cut out
- the ways these fabrics are joined together
- additional constructional techniques which affect the shape of the cut-out pieces.

It also describes the effect of cutting on the bias.

The next part of the chapter deals with the skills needed to make garments and similar items. The aim is to provide students with the information to choose the most appropriate making process and the correct tools and equipment when they are making their products. Clearly the information will not impart the tacit know-how required to use these techniques safely

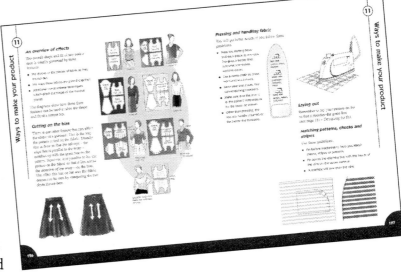

and effectively. There is no substitute for clear skill instruction and the opportunity to practise, so it is important that you use sound demonstration linked to appropriate Resource Tasks to enable students to increase their making skills.

The following important making processes are described:

- pressing and handling fabric
- hand sewing and stitches
- machine sewing
- joining and shaping: seams, tucks and pleats, gathering, darts, sleeve fitting
- opening and fastenings
- casings
- edges, middles and other bits: shaped facings, waistbands, pockets and collars.

The final part of this chapter deals with the specialist construction techniques needed for tents and kites.

Chapter 12 Health and safety

This chapter revisits the important ideas established earlier – hazards, risks, risk assessment and risk control – and uses them in looking at unfamiliar situations: a weaving plant and a textile garment production factory.

5 Using Capability Tasks

Specifying a Capability Task

The Nuffield Project has identified the following 14 features which describe a Capability Task and the associated learning for 14–16 year-olds. It is based on the successful model used earlier but four of the features are new.

1 **The task** A short statement which indicates the type of product that the students will design and make.

2 **Task setting** It is important that the task is placed in a setting that can be investigated in a way that informs the subsequent designing and making. The investigation should answer the following questions:

- Whom is the product for?
- What is it for?
- Where will it be used?
- When will it be used?
- Is it a one-off or is it to be mass produced?
- Where might it be sold?
- Who is likely to buy it?

3 **The aims of the task** These will indicate what is to be taught through the task. This will be linked to the type of product that the students will design and make and usually includes four features:

- learning and using some strategies;
- learning and using some technical knowledge and understanding;
- learning and using some communication techniques;
- learning and using some making skills.

4 **Values** It is important for students to appreciate the values that inform the nature of the need or opportunity and to find ways to take them into account. This is more complex than **5** and **6** as the detail of the value considerations will depend on the nature of the task setting. This will be revealed by the students' investigation of the setting and for this they will need appropriate strategies. These will be detailed in a Programme of Study or syllabus and can be taught through an appropriate set or sequence of Resource Tasks (see **9**). It will be important for students to consider their own values and move towards a recognition and understanding of the values of others. They will need to think about situations where there are value conflicts and move from simple two-sided arguments to understanding complex conflicts involving many-sided arguments. Arguments where qualitative values, for example aesthetic considerations, are in conflict with quantitative values, for example economic considerations, are probably the most difficult to resolve. The values are presented under the following headings:

- technical • economic • aesthetic • moral • social • environmental.

They do not represent mutually exclusive sets and there will often be overlap between the categories. Reading and thinking about Case Studies is a useful way to develop values thinking (see **10**).

5 **Nature of the product** This has three sections.
From the exploration which lists a selection of written work that should be developed through the initial stages of the task. This always includes a preliminary specification.
For the production and promotion which lists a selection of written work that should be developed to ensure promotion/marketing of the product and quality assured production. To meet this last feature it always requires a detailed specification which includes textiles, equipment and production schedule.
Possible products which describes the sort of product that the students will design and make at a level of detail that indicates the knowledge, understanding and skills likely to be required. For example a glove puppet is a simple product even with string hair, embroidered features and hands modelled in fymo. Designing and making this is a modest task. A full-size puppet suit for characters like those in *Sesame Street* is a much more demanding affair. There is a dynamic relationship between the nature of the product and the knowledge and understanding of technical matters and making skill. Complex products *demand* high-level knowledge and skill; high-level knowledge and skill *lead* to complex products.

6 **Technical knowledge and understanding** This is related to the nature of the product the students are designing and making and can be referenced against the Programme of Study or syllabus and taught through an appropriate set or sequence of Resource Tasks (see **9**).

7 **Specialist tools, materials and equipment** For 14–16 year-olds it is assumed that most general-purpose tools and equipment will be available. Only specialist or unusual items will be noted. Similarly with fabrics and fastenings only the uncommon will be detailed.

8 **Cross-curricular links** The use of other areas of knowledge and understanding should be such that they aid the students' designing and making. The approach of, say, science to a particular area – such as the properties of materials – may stress quantifiable data obtained through testing. However, a different approach by the design and technology teacher, concentrating perhaps on an intuitive response to the tactile and visual qualities of fabrics, may seem in conflict with the scientific approach and only serve to confuse the pupil. So it will be important to check with colleagues in other curriculum areas and try to use consistent and complementary approaches.

The cross-curricular links are summarized using headings which indicate a particular subject or theme, for example using art, or using economic and industrial understanding.

9 **Useful Resource Tasks** A listing of relevant Resource Tasks is always provided. Only you will know which ones are appropriate for your students. Depending on their previous experience and learning they may need to do all of the suggested tasks, some or only a few. In a very few cases a student may not need to do any but this is likely to be a rare exception as an important feature of capability is the ability to use new knowledge, understanding and skill.

10 **Useful Case Studies** A listing of relevant Case Studies is always provided. Only you will know which ones are appropriate for your students or how best to use them – with the whole class, with a small group or with an individual. They do provide an important opportunity for the student to reflect on the wider issues of design and technology as well as more focused work concerning quality and products and applications.

A clear description of **1–10** above provides a detailed specification for a Capability Task. This whole approach makes it clear what you have to teach for students to become capable in design and technology. It is only when the teaching requirements are clear that you can organize lessons so that learning can take place. However, in order to enable you to modify the tasks and start them at different points in from the usual beginning point, the following features are also described.

11 Design brief This will always describe some or all of the following features:

- the sort of product that is to be made and its purpose;
- who will use it;
- where it will be used;
- where it might be sold.

12 Preliminary specification This will always describe the following features:

- what it should do;
- what it should look like;
- other features such as:
  - how it should work;
  - how much it should cost to manufacture, or limiting the cost of starting materials;
  - possible production levels: one-off or batch;
  - from what materials it should be made;
  - ergonomic requirements related to the end user;
  - legal requirements to be met in its development;
  - environmental considerations and requirements.

13 Possible associated activities This section makes suggestions as to activities that do not fall into the Case Study/Resource Task categories that you might wish to include in the task. It is here that opportunities for visits and visiting speakers are noted.

14 Design sketches These will give an impression of one or two products that could be made in response to the brief and specification. There is insufficient information for the student to make the product without some more design input.

15 Information for making These will deal with simple rather than complex products. They will be in the form of an exploded view of the item plus a simple pattern which can be used as a starting point for design. There will be insufficient information to make the item without further design input.

How the Capability Tasks are presented

Capability Tasks for 14–16 year-olds are presented as copy master A4 overview sheets so that the information is easily and rapidly accessible.

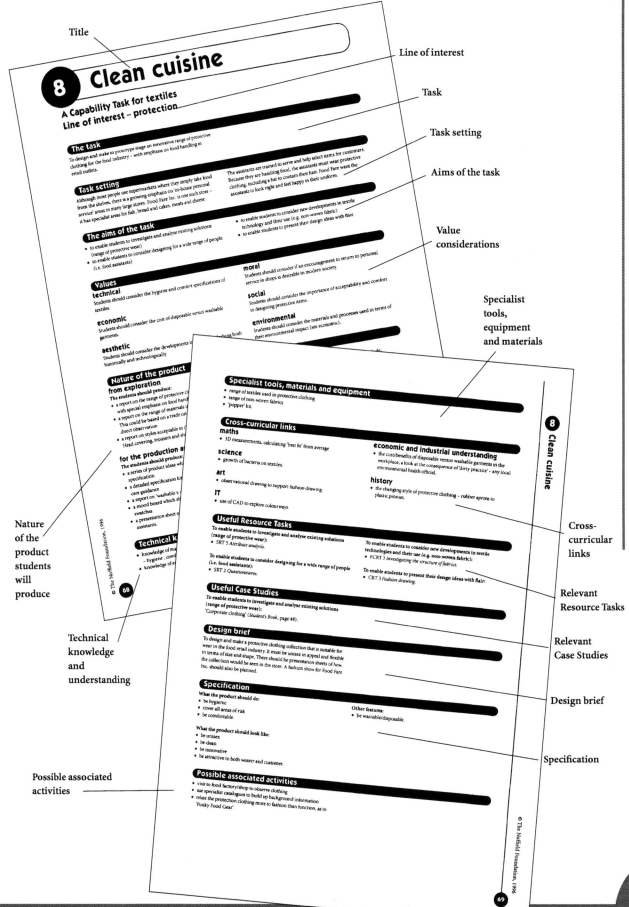

Using Capability Tasks

Using the Capability Tasks to plan a full GCSE course

Managing three Capability Tasks

It is likely that your students will tackle three Capability Tasks during year 10, each one from a different line of interest. You can work out which ones your class will tackle. In year 11, students can revisit a line of interest or tackle a new one. The one in year 11 will probably be used for their GCSE course work. This makes sense because the students should be better at designing and making in year 11 than they were in year 10. It will be quite a struggle to fit three complete Capability Tasks into year 10 so you may wish to organize the lessons so that students do only part of some of these tasks. They will certainly need to do one complete Capability Task where they design, make and test a well-finished product. There are several ways to shorten Capability Tasks.

- You might shorten it so that the students produce only a paper toile plus swatches. This means that the time spent is reduced as the students don't have to spend a lot of time making the finished article.

- You might decide that the students should produce only a series of design proposals as detailed annotated sketches. This cuts down the time they spend on the Capability Task even further.

- You may decide to give the class a design brief plus a specification and ask them to design and make a product that meets these requirements. This removes all of the task setting investigation from the task, brief and specification development and so lessens the time spent.

- You could decide to give the class the brief, specification and some design sketches as a starting point. This will cut down the design development phase even further.

- You might even give the class the brief, the specification and a basic pattern and ask them to make the product because, for example, they need to concentrate on manufacturing. This will reduce the time spent even further.

Example briefs, specifications, design sketches and simple patterns are included in Part 2 of this Guide so that you have control over the time spent on the tasks. Of course, it is important that the students still carry out the Resource Tasks and Case Studies needed for each of the Capability Tasks. In this way they can acquire a great deal of design and technology knowledge, understanding and skill and still keep in touch with designing and making. This will put the students in a strong position to tackle a full Capability Task in year 11. It is important that the students know at the outset of the Capability Task how long it is going to take and in what way it will be shortened from being a full Capability Task. They need to be quite clear about the expected outcomes. There is little that is more disappointing for a student than to start a Capability Task with the expectation of taking home a finished piece only to be told during the task 'Well, we haven't got time to finish so your fashion drawings will do'.

If you are teaching a **short course** you will need to reduce the number of Capability Tasks accordingly and perhaps complete just one full and one reduced-time task before students tackle their main task for GCSE assessment.

5 Choosing the lines of interest

The lines of interest have been chosen because they represent different degrees of risk as far as the teacher is concerned. Some of the lines of interest involve students designing and making products with which most teachers are quite familiar and the likelihood of the students being successful is high. This is simply because the teacher is so familiar with the knowledge, understanding and skills required for success and the typical pitfalls, that he or she can teach appropriately to the task and provide effective guidance without the student losing ownership of the work.

Other lines of interest are slightly less safe and the majority of teachers may feel some concern about the level of success they can guarantee with students designing and making these sorts of product. Some other lines of interest may be seen as high risk in that they are outside the previous experience of the teacher. Exactly what constitutes a risk to you and the level of that risk will depend on your specialist training, any in-service training you may have received, the facilities in your school and your previous teaching experience. While only you can make the best judgement, the Nuffield Project offers the following guidance.

Of the three Capability Tasks you might teach in year 10, choose two that are low risk. In this way the bulk of your work in year 10 is likely to be successful. If for some reason you are not successful in this area of risk then the damage is easy to limit. If, however, you are successful, this is good professional development and over a period of time this part of your teaching will cease to be one of risk and become an area of guaranteed success. You will then be in a position to tackle a further and different area of risk in the knowledge that you can be successful.

Assessment 6

In-built assessment through reviewing

It is important that your students work in a way that reveals their design and technology thinking. Evidence of their capability should emerge quite naturally from the way they tackle a Capability Task. The way students review the progress of their work during a Capability Task is an important means of providing you with assessment evidence. From the student's viewpoint reviewing is essential for two reasons. Firstly, it demands that the student stop and reflect on what has been done so far and the consequences of this for further action. Thus it is an important strategy in giving students a sense that designing is a coherent and continuous activity; that the activity is not a series of unconnected steps prompted, perhaps, by teacher intervention or worksheet instruction. It is important for students to view designing as a sequence of connected activities over which they have some control. Reviewing helps to establish this view. Secondly, in confronting students with the consequences of their actions, the review procedure can provide momentum for the task in that it forces students to make decisions about what to do next.

In one sense reviewing should be happening continuously as every action should be the result of a plan–execute–review cycle.

- I plan to take a particular course of action because . . .

- I do it.

- I reflect on the result of the doing (i.e. I review the consequences of my actions) and use these thoughts to plan my next actions, and so on.

It is quite impossible to monitor this continuous and on-going reviewing within a student's work but the Nuffield Project has identified the following three staging posts in design activity where a more formal review is extremely useful.

First review

Once students have some ideas for their products in the form of quickly drawn annotated sketches they should then carry out their first review by comparing their ideas with the requirements of the brief and the specification. They should ask themselves the following questions for each design idea:

- Will the design do what it is supposed to?

- Will the design be suitable for the users?

- Will the design fit in with where it might be used or sold?

- Is the design likely to work?

- Does the design look right for the users and sellers?

- Have I noted any special requirements the design will need to meet later on?

Any design ideas that do not get a 'yes' for all these questions will need to be rejected or adjusted. In this way students can use the first review to screen out any design ideas that will not meet their requirements. They can do this screening in two ways: as an individual by just sitting, thinking it through and making notes against each design idea; or they can work in a group and explain their ideas to other students who can check them out against the questions. This latter method takes longer and each student has to help the others in the group check out their design ideas. But the extra time is usually well spent as the overall level of constructive criticism is higher. Whichever way you choose for your students to review their work, it is important that they discuss their review findings with you.

Second review

By screening their early ideas students will be able to focus their efforts into developing a single design idea and work out the details of that design. They will present these details as a mixture of thumbnail sketches, cutouts, annotated drawings, toiles, swatch collections and patterns.

To make sure that their designing is still developing in a sensible direction, they need to ask the following questions before they begin making the product.

- Am I sure that the working parts of the design will do what they are supposed to?
- Am I sure about the accuracy with which I need to make each part?
- How long will it take me to make and assemble all the parts of my design?
- Have I got enough time to do this?
- If not, what can I alter so that I have a design that I can make on time and that still meets the specification?
- Will the materials I need be available when I need them?
- Will the tools and equipment be available when I need them?
- Am I sure that I can get the final appearance that I need?
- Have I got enough time for finishing?
- Is there anything I can do to be more efficient?

The individual student is probably the only one who can answer these questions but it is important that you establish the routine where they check their answers with you in order to avoid hidden traps and pitfalls.

Third review

Once the design has been produced the students should review their products to check performance against specification, user reaction, winner/loser balance and appropriateness. There are Resource Tasks which revise these methods of evaluation and it is important to make these product evaluation sessions active. One way to do this is for you to organize students into discussion groups. Each student gives his/her product a blob score for each part of the specification – five blobs if it meets that part really well, three if it meets it moderately well, one if it meets it only poorly and none if it fails to meet this part of the specification. Each student, in turn, then explains to the other students in the group why these scores have been given. The rest of the group questions these judgements. Each student has to convince the others that the judgements are correct. This activity is a powerful incentive to look at overall progress.

Students looking at their own progress

At the end of a Capability Task it is important for students to look back at what they have done and reflect on their progress. The *Student's Book* contains the following sets of questions to help students do this.

Feeling good about what you have done

- Am I proud of what I have made?
- Can I explain why?
- Am I proud of the design I developed?
- Can I explain why?

Understanding the problems

- What sort of things slowed me down?
- Can I now see how to overcome these sorts of difficulty?
- What sort of things made me nervous so that I didn't do as well as I know I can?
- Do I know where to get help now?
- What sort of things did I do better than I expected?
- Was this due to luck or can I say that I'm getting better?
- Were there times when I concentrated on detail before I had the broad picture?
- Were there times when I didn't bother enough with detail?
- Can I now see how to get the level of detail right?

Understanding yourself

- Were there times when I lost interest?
- Can I now see how to get myself motivated?
- Were there times when I couldn't work out what to do next?
- Can I now see how to get better at making decisions?
- Were there times when I lost my sense of direction?
- Can I now see how to avoid this?

Understanding your design decisions

- With hindsight can I see where I made the right decisions?
- With hindsight can I see where I should have made different decisions?
- With hindsight can I see situations where I did the right thing?
- With hindsight can I see where I would do things differently if I did this again?

You can use students' answers to these questions to see strengths and weaknesses and to identify areas for improvement.

6 Examination questions

The Nuffield Project has identified eight types of questions which may be set for GCSE written, terminal examinations. It is important that you are familiar with these and teach your students to respond appropriately to each type.

Type 1: knowledge definitions

The candidate is expected to show understanding of key terms, principles and concepts. The question will be written in a form which requires candidates to *recognize* or *give an example* which illustrates the meaning, but does not expect candidates to be able to recall and state a definition.

Example

A local café, called 'Coffee Time', has asked you to design a new logo to use on its menu. It wants the logo to *appeal* to its customers.

For recognition

Imagine you are writing a questionnaire to check which of your two logo designs is more *appealing*. Which of the following questions would you include?

- Which logo looks more interesting?
- Which logo would 'Coffee Time' like better?
- Which logo would make you want to buy a coffee?
- Which logo do you like?

For giving examples

Imagine you need to write a questionnaire to check which of your two logo designs is more *appealing*. Suggest three suitable questions.

Both could be extended to ask students to *explain* their choices, and describe *methods* of carrying out the survey, collecting and presenting results.

Type 2: knowledge of purpose (Why?)

The candidate is expected to show understanding of:

- why things are done in a particular way (Why do it in that way?);
- why actions or decisions are significant or important (Why would you do 'x' or why is it like that?);
- why decisions are appropriate or have been made (Why has it been made from 'x'?).

The question will be written in a form which asks the student to explain or justify.

Example

The candidate will be given information about a product in the form of annotated illustrations and text. He/she will be asked to explain different features of the design such as:

- why a particular fabric has been chosen;
- why a part is the shape and form that it is.

This could be extended to ask students to explain *method*, or to *predict* effects of changed variables, or to make a *creative response*.

Type 3: knowledge of method (How?)

The candidate is expected to describe or explain showing understanding of:

- processes, materials and techniques (How could I make this design from particular materials?);
- the application of technological principles (show how you would do 'x' or make 'x' happen);
- the application of design strategies (How would you research, analyse, review, make decisions, plan, test, evaluate, etc?).

The question will be written in a form which asks students to *describe* using a suitable mode of response, such as notes and diagrams, grid/matrix or flow chart.

Example

The candidate will be given information about a product in the form of annotated illustrations and text and asked:

- the order in which the item might be assembled;
- how the fabric might be decorated;
- how risks can be avoided when using a necessary technique;
- how the product could be adapted to make it more easy to use;
- how to test a particular part for weather resistance;
- how to carry out a user trip;
- how to calculate costs of making.

Type 4: speculating about change (What if?)

The candidate will be asked to predict the results of given changes in circumstances or variables, including:

- the direct consequences of things (What would happen if you did 'x'?);
- the effect on connected things (If you changed 'x' then what effect would this have on 'y'?).

The question will be written in a form which asks the student to *suggest what would happen if*.

Example

The candidate will be presented with a diagram showing the layout and dimensions of main sections on folded 900 mm width fabric, and a sketch of finished shorts. They will be required to 'Imagine you are working out how much fabric you will need to make a pair of shorts. You have planned your layout for a length of fabric that was 900 mm wide.' The candidate may then be asked to …

- *Consider a direct consequence* You could not get the colour you wanted in 900 mm width, it is available only in 1540 mm width.
- Say whether you will need more or less fabric and show how you worked out your answer.
- *Consider an indirect consequence* You have decided to get the 900 mm wide fabric and dye it to get the colour you want.
- List the main stages needed to produce the shorts from fabric which does not need to be dyed.
- Show how this plan would change.

Type 5: creative problem-solving

The candidate will be asked to develop a *personal response* to a short technical design problem. The question will be written in a form which requires students to *suggest* possible solutions, *compare* their alternatives, select and *justify a recommended* solution.

Example

The candidate will be presented with an incomplete design to which there are several different possible solutions. Three questions might then be asked, such as the following.

- Use notes and sketches to illustrate two possible solutions to the problem.
- Make a list for each of your ideas to show the strengths and weaknesses of your solutions.
- State clearly which idea you think is the best and give your reasons.

It is here that some formal requirements to use mathematics or science can be included in the question.

Type 6: design strategies

The candidate will be asked to use design *strategies* on a short design scenario. The question will be written in a form which requires the student to *use a given strategy* to carry out design analysis, development or evaluation. Strategies could include:

- clarifying briefs – turning an open-ended brief into a more specific form;
- writing specifications – turning a headline specification into a more detailed form;
- attribute analysis – analysing possible product characteristics;
- brainstorming – completing a started brainstorm or organizing a random list from a brainstorm to show categories and links;
- impact of D&T – interrogating a completed winners and losers chart;
- user trip – interpreting user views and opinions.

Example

The candidate will be presented with a series of images showing the reactions of someone using a product. For example, trying on a hat: image 1 – looking at the hat, image 2 – looking in a mirror, image 3 – hat in a different position, image 4 – talking to a friend and pointing at the hat, and so on.

The candidate will be told that these photos were taken of someone testing a new hat which was designed to . . . (simple brief) . . .

The candidate will be asked the following.

- Write down what you think they were asked to do.
- How do you think this person responded to the product?
- Write down the reactions of the person testing the product.

Type 7: presenting and interpreting information

The candidate will be asked to make sense of D&T research data. The question will be written in a form which requires a student

- to *present* the information clearly;
- to *interpret* the data and reach conclusions.

Example

The candidate will be given data from some design and technology research, which may come from very different sources. It could be about:

- consumer preferences about indoor slippers, say;
- the results of testing a fabric or fastening;
- production figures for different manufacturing methods;
- sales figures for different products.

For presenting

- Draw a graph or chart to show what people of different age groups thought about the old version of the indoor slippers as compared with the new version.
- Think carefully about which would be the most appropriate form of graph or chart to use to present the data clearly.

For interpreting

- Which age group of consumers has changed its views most about indoor slippers?
- Write down which you think and give reasons for your view.

Type 8: interpreting a short Case Study

The candidate will be asked to use *comprehension* skills, design *strategies* and *knowledge* to demonstrate their *understanding* of design and technology activity from the world outside school. The question will be written in a form which requires the student

- to *find a piece of information* from the text;
- to *explain* something that is described in the text;
- to *make judgements* about the quality and effects of the design and technology described.

It is here also that the application of science or mathematics may be built into the question.

Example

The Case Study could present information about the way fashions in men's shirts have changed over the past 60 years. The candidate could be asked

- to *find information*
  - When were drip-dry shirts introduced to this country?
  - What fibres are present in drip-dry fabrics?

- to *explain design and technology understanding*
  - Explain the advantages and disadvantages of shirts with separate collars compared with attached collars.
  - Explain the use of built-in stiffenings compared to the use of starch.
  - Explain the differing levels of automation used in manufacturing the fabric and the shirt.

- to *make judgements*
  - Explain why some people are critical of consumers buying new clothes because their current clothes have become unfashionable rather than worn out.
  - Explain why some groups support textile recycling schemes.

Different Examination Boards 7

This chapter provides a brief summary of the requirements of different Examination Boards and indicates those syllabuses that are supported by Nuffield materials.

City and Guilds of London Institute

Courses being offered

The following are being offered as both full and short GCSE courses:
  Design and Technology (unendorsed – two focus areas)
  Design and Technology: Resistant Materials Technology ✓
  Design and Technology: Food Technology ✓
  Design and Technology: Textile Technology ✓
  Design and Technology: Graphic Products ✓
  Design and Technology: Electronic Products ✓

A combined course in Design and Technology and Business Enterprise will also be offered.

✓ Are supported by Nuffield materials

Course work requirements

This is in two parts:

- candidates are required to produce an integrated design and make project duration approximately 20 hours for a short course or 40 hours for a full course;

- candidates are required to produce a written product evaluation report on an existing product.

Course work accounts for 60% of the total marks (one third for designing, two thirds for making) and will be moderated by external moderators visiting the centre.

Examination requirements

For the short course candidates are required to take a 1.25 hour examination based on section A of the syllabus.

For the full course candidates are required to take the same 1.25 hours examination as the short course candidates plus a further paper of 1.25 hours based on section B of the syllabus. The examination counts for 40% of the total marks (50% designing, 50% making); there are two tiers for written papers: A*–D and C–G.

Key features

- Allows candidates to specialize in a single materials focus area or work in two focus areas.

- Provides a teacher support guide.

- Links with GNVQs at Foundation and Intermediate levels.

- Detailed assessment course work grid with criteria for each GCSE grade.

- External moderator support.

- Specified requirements of design applications in an industrial context.

- Prepares students for the technological world requiring them to design and make products in response to needs and opportunities.

For further information contact:
  Subject Officer, 46 Britannia Street, London, WC1X 9RG
  Tel: 0171 294 2468 Fax: 0171 294 2400

31

Midland Examining Group

Courses being offered

The following are being offered as both full and short GCSE courses:
- D&T: Resistant Materials Technology ✓
- D&T: Textile Technology ✓
- D&T: Graphic Products ✓
- D&T: Electronic Products ✓
- D&T: Food Technology ✓

The following are being offered as full GCSE courses only:
- D&T: Systems and Control Products
- D&T: Automotive Engineering.

D&T Engineering is offered as both full and dual award.

✓ Are supported by Nuffield materials

Course work requirements

All course work has an overall weighting of 60%. For syllabuses offered as both full and short GCSE courses candidates are required to complete a course work project – a design folder and realization of a quality product. For the full course this represents 40/60 hours of curriculum time and for the short course 20/30 hours.

For D&T Systems and Control Products candidates are required to complete a course work project – a design folder and the realization of a system/control product. For D&T Automotive Engineering candidates are required to complete a course work project – a design folder and the realization of a system/control product (40%) and practical assignments (20%). For D&T Engineering candidates are required to produce a portfolio selection of work. In addition, dual aware candidates will have to complete a response to an Engineering Design Brief and an Engineering Report.

Examination requirements

All terminal examinations have an overall weighting of 40%. There are two tiers of entry:
Higher – A* to D (U)   Foundation – C to G

For the syllabuses being offered as both full and short GCSE courses candidates taking a short course take one paper; candidates taking a full course take two papers.

For D&T: Systems and Control Products candidates take two papers – Paper 1: Core, Paper 2: Option. For D&T: Automotive Engineering candidates take one paper. For D&T: Engineering candidates complete a Board set Capability Task (Duration 10 hours), and take one paper for the single award or two papers for the dual award.

Key features

- All course work internally assessed and standardized, moderation will be by visit.
- Allows candidates to produce a realistic product for course work.
- New, 'user friendly' course work assessment scheme.
- Full INSET programme commenced October 1995.

For further information contact:
Subject Officer, Midlands Examining Group, Robins Wood House, Robins Wood Road, Aspley, Nottingham, NG8 3NR Tel: 0115 929 6021 Fax: 0115 929 5261

Northern Examinations and Assessment Board

Courses being offered

The following are being offered as both full and short GCSE courses:
  Design and Technology: Resistant Materials ✓
  Design and Technology: Graphic Products ✓
  Design and Technology: Food Technolog ✓
  Design and Technology: Textile Technology ✓
  Design and Technology: Electronic Products ✓

The following is being offered as full GCSE courses only:
  Design and Technology: Systems
  ✓Are supported by Nuffield materials

Course work requirements

Course work submission is 60% of the overall assessment (20% designing and 40% making). Candidates are required to complete a major project consisting of a design folder and a practical outcome. The project will be assessed holistically using the two assessment objectives, Designing and Making.

The time to be spent on the project will depend on the material area. The short course requirements are half those for the full course, e.g., Design and Technology: Textile Technology about 50/25 hours, Design and Technology: Food Technology 25/12 hours.

Examination requirements

Examination counts for 40% of the total marks. All candidates sit a single written paper, set at two tiers, with separate papers for the full and short course.

For the full course Higher level candidates (Grades A*–D) take a written paper of 2.5 hours and Foundation level candidates (Grades C–G) take a 2 hour written paper.

For the short course Higher level candidates (Grades A*–D) take a written paper for 2 hours and Foundation level candidates (Grades C–G) take a 1.5 hour written paper.

Key features

- All syllabuses build on the good practice developed in the current Design and Technology syllabuses.

- Each syllabus may be delivered by an individual teacher.

- Common syllabus section based on Key Stage 4 Design and Technology Programme of Study for designing and making.

- Moderation is by inspection, normally by visiting moderators.

- Teachers will be supported by meetings, both before teaching starts and during the course.

For further information contact:
  Subject Officer, NEAB, Wheatfield Road, Westerhope, Newcastle-upon-tyne, NE5 5JZ
  Tel: 0191 201 0180 Fax: 0191 271 3314

RSA Examinations Board

Courses being offered

The following are being offered as both full and short GCSE courses:
- Design and Technology (unendorsed, multi-material, covering Resistant Materials)✓
- Design and Technology: Textiles Technology ✓
- Design and Technology: Food Technology ✓
- Design and Technology: Graphical Products ✓

✓ Are supported by Nuffield materials

Course work requirements

Course work accounts for 60% of the total marks (one third for designing, two thirds for making) and will be moderated by externally-appointed moderators visiting the centre.

Candidates are required to produce a portfolio of work including a substantial designing and making task. The substantial task should take approximately 20 hours for the short course and approximately 40 hours for the full course.

Examination requirements

Examination counts for 40% of the total marks divided equally between designing and making.

For the short course candidates are required to take a one hour examination based on a scenario set by RSA in advance of the examination which will draw on the knowledge, skills and understanding identified for the GCSE (short course) including the chosen manufacturing material area.

For the full course, in addition to taking the same one hour examination as the short course candidates, candidates will take a further one hour extension paper to show more detailed knowledge and understanding of working with a design specification in the industrial manufacturing material area they have chosen.

Key features

- Provides full teacher support including a support pack and INSET.
- Allows credit towards GNVQ Intermediate Manufacturing Units.

For further information contact:
Subject Officer, RSA Examination Board, Westward Way, Coventry, West Midlands CV4 8HS Tel: 01203 470033 Fax: 01203 468080

Southern Examining Group

Courses being offered

Both full and short courses are offered.

The Design and Technology full course syllabus (3400) consists of two parts: 1) a common syllabus section and 2) an area of focus.

Candidates choose from one of the following areas of focus:

Electronic Products ✓
Graphic Products ✓
Systems and Control Products
Product Design and Manufacture ✓
Food Technology ✓
Textile Technology ✓

The Design and Technology short course (1400) consists of the common syllabus section only without the areas of focus.

✓ Are supported by Nuffield materials

Course work requirements

Course work submission is 60% of the overall assessment (40% for designing skills, 60% for making skills). Candidates are required to submit an assignment integrating designing and making supported by additional tasks, or alternatively two integrated assignments. Course work submission may be achieved through the common syllabus content and one area of focus. Moderation will be by area moderation meetings under the direction of a SEG moderator.

Examination requirements

The written papers of the examination are 40% of the overall assessment (40% for designing and 60% for making).

For the full course candidates are required to take a written paper of 1.5 hours on the common syllabus section and a written paper of 1 hour on their chosen area of focus.

For the short course candidates are required to take a written paper of 1.5 hours on the common syllabus section.

Key features

- Common syllabus section based on Key Stage 4 Programme of Study for Design and Technology.

- Builds upon the Key Stage 3 Programme of Study for Design and Technology.

- Allows centres a flexible approach to the subject.

- Provides specimen question papers and marking scheme.

- Provides a comprehensive teacher support package, including printed exemplar materials, regional support meetings and experienced staff for dealing with queries.

For further information contact:

Subject Officer, Southern Examining Group, Staghill House, Guildford, Surrey, GU2 5XJ
Tel: 01483 506506 Fax: 01483 300152

University of London Examinations & Assessment Council

The following are being offered as both full and short GCSE courses:
  Design and Technology: Product Design ✓
  Design and Technology: Graphic Products ✓
  Design and Technology: Electronic Products ✓
  Design and Technology: Food Technology ✓
  Design and Technology: Textile Technology ✓
The following combined course is being offered:
  Design and Technology: Product Design and Business.
  ✓ Are supported by Nuffield materials

Course work requirements

Course work accounts for 60% of the total marks for both full and short courses.

For the full course, candidates will have to produce one major Capability Task (40%) taking approximately 30 hours and an assignment (20%) taking approximately 10 hours.

For the short course: candidates will have to produce one major Capability Task (40%) taking approximately 15 hours and an assignment (20%) taking approximately 5 hours.

Themes for the tasks will be chosen by candidates and approved by teachers in accordance with their chosen focus area and lines of interest. ULEAC will provide exemplar material to guide teachers in selecting and setting tasks.

Examination requirements

The written papers of the examination are 40% of the overall assessment.
  The full course examination lasts 2.5 hours.
  The short course examination lasts 1.5 hours.

Key features

- Each syllabus has a single focus area which allows candidates to develop their skills of designing and making and their knowledge and understanding in a field of special interest to them.

- The skills, knowledge and understanding of this syllabus may be realized in a variety of contexts, according to the resources available and the interests of teacher and candidates.

- The Council will provide teacher support and guidance for the course work and for the syllabus.

For further information contact

  Subject Officer, ULEAC, Stewart House, 32 Russell Square, London, WC1B 5DN
  Tel: 0171 331 4000 Fax: 0171 753 4558

Welsh Joint Education Committee

Courses being offered

Design and Technology is being offered as full, combined and short GCSE courses in the five combined syllabuses. Design and Technology may be taken with either Art, Business Studies, Catering, Electronics or Information Technology.

All courses may be delivered through one or more of the following six focus areas:

- Control
- Food ✓
- Graphic Media ✓
- Product Design ✓
- Resistant Materials ✓
- Textiles ✓

✓ Are supported by Nuffield materials

Course work requirements

Course work submission is 60% of the overall assessment and there is a 40 : 60 weighting between designing and making.

For a full course candidates are required to complete a single substantial design and make project, which may be based on one or more of the focus areas.

For a short course candidates are required to complete a single substantial design and make project, which may be based on one or more of the focus areas but the depth of study and time commitment of the project is reduced compared to the full course.

Project work will be assessed by the centre and a sample moderated by a visiting examiner.

Examination requirements and weightings

The written papers of the examination are 40% of the overall assessment. For the full course there will be a terminal examination consisting of two papers, totalling 2.5 hours duration:

- Paper 1 is common to all focus areas.

- Paper 2 is specific to a single focus area – candidates select one from six.

Candidates will be required to demonstrate designing skills and an understanding of making skills applicable to at least one of the focus areas.

For short and combined courses candidates sit only Paper 1.

Key features

- There are two tiers of entry: Foundation – C to G, Higher – A* to D.

- Develops candidates' competence to address a wide variety of design situations by drawing upon a broad base of knowledge and skills.

- The syllabus provides the opportunity for a number of existing curriculum areas to make a contribution to the examination.

- The syllabus is sufficiently broad, balanced and relevant to interest all candidates.

For further information contact:
Subject Officer, Welsh Joint Education Committee, 245 Western Avenue, Cardiff Wales, CF5 2YX Tel: 01222 265000 Fax: 01222 575994

8 Resource Task Summary Tables

Task number and title	Learning	Type of task	Links with other subjects	Time	Demand	Capability Tasks supported
SRT 1 Identifying needs and likes	To identify needs and likes	Recap		Part 1: 40 minutes Part 2: 40 minutes	*	Travel safe, Feely bags unlimited, Audition kit bag, Happy cotton, Squashy seats, Snuggly buggly
SRT 2 Using a database	How to make use of information collected in a survey How to use a database to handle the information	New	IT	120 minutes	***	Clean cuisine, Home comforts, Happy cotton, Squashy seats
SRT 3 Design briefs and specifications	To extend your understanding of how to: Part 1: write design briefs in response to needs, wants and likes Part 2: write a specification from a design brief	Extension		Part 1: 40 minutes Part 2: 40 minutes	**	Squashy seats, Can be used with any Capability Tasks as appropriate
SRT 4 Brainstorming	To apply two sorts of brainstorming	Extension		Part 1: 40 minutes Part 2: 40 minutes	**	Travel safe, Home comforts, Feely bags unlimited, Squashy seats, Snuggly buggly
SRT 5 Attribute analysis	To extend your understanding of how to use attribute analysis to think up different ideas for a product	Extension		45 minutes	**	Clean cuisine, Themed scarves, Feely bags unlimited, Snuggly buggly, Squashy Seats
SRT 6 Evaluating	To extend your understanding of how to evaluate a design by thinking how it affects people, whether it performs as expected and whether it is appropriate	Extension		Part 1: 40 minutes Part 2: 40 minutes	**	Can be used with any Capability Tasks as appropriate
SRT 7 Systems and control	Application of systems and control concepts to textile product manufacture	Extension		40 minutes	***	Can be used with any Capability Tasks as appropriate
CRT 1 Mood boards and theme boards	To use mood or theme boards to communicate a design idea	Extension	Art	90 minutes	*	Themed scarves, Customized carriers, A cast of thousands, Audition kit bag, Happy cotton, Rap wrap, Character hotels, Kite bonanza
CRT 2 Presenting data	To present data in an easily accessible form	Extension	IT	60 minutes	**	A cast of thousands, Happy cotton
CRT 3 Fashion drawing	To present ideas for fashion clothes	New	Art	90 minutes	***	Clean cuisine, A cast of thousands, Audition kit bag, Rap wrap

Resource Task Summary Tables

Task number and title	Learning	Type of task	Links with other subjects	Time	Demand	Capability Tasks supported
CRT 4 Capturing fabric on paper	To draw items made from fabric in a realistic way	New	Art	90 minutes	***	Travel safe, Home comforts, Customized carriers, Feely bags unlimited, Character hotels, Snuggly buggly, Kite bonanza
CRT 5 Exploring interiors	To show the effect of different textile products on an interior	New	IT	120 minutes	**	Character hotels, A cast of thousands, Audition kit bag
CRT 6 Communicating ideas to the maker	To ensure that information for making textile items is complete	New		60 minutes	**	Customized carriers, Feely bags unlimited, A cast of thousands, Audition kit bag, Travel safe, Home comforts, Rap wrap, Snuggly buggly, Kite bonanza
DRT 1 Tie-dyeing with natural dyes – an investigation	To carry out tie-dyeing and investigate natural dyes	Recap and extension		120 minutes	**	Character hotels
DRT 2 Batik snowflakes	To use batik to decorate a small square of fabric that can be made into a scarf or head band	New	Mathematics	120 minutes	**	Themed scarves, Character hotels, Kite bonanza
FCRT 1 Layering	To construct fabric by layering	Extension		120 minutes	**	Character hotels
FCRT 2 Knitting to make textured buttons	To produce fabric by knitting and use the fabric for covering buttons	New	Mathematics	120 minutes	**	Feely bags unlimited
FCRT 3 Investigating the structure of fabrics	How the structure of a fabric affects its properties	Extension		60 minutes	***	Clean cuisine, Squashy seats
HSRT 1 Health and safety	To revise and extend understanding of how to be safe, and ensure the safety of others	Recap and extension		40 minutes	**	Can be used with any Capability Tasks as appropriate
MfRT 1 Rally arm bands	To design and make a batch of simple textile products	New		180 minutes	**	Themed scarves

Resource Task Summary Tables

Task number and title	Learning	Type of task	Links with other subjects	Time	Demand	Capability Tasks supported
LIRT 1 Fashion accessories: weaving a small bag	To use weaving to construct a fabric	New	Mathematics	120 minutes	**	Home comforts
LIRT 2 Bags and carriers: simple bag decorated with block printing	To construct a simple fabric bag and decorate it with block printing	New	IT	240 minutes	**	Themed scarves, Customized carriers, Happy cotton, Character hotels
LIRT 3 Interiors: wall hanging for a child's bedroom	To make felt, decorate it with embroidery stitches and use it for appliqué	New		180 minutes	**	Rap wrap, Character hotels
LIRT 4 Kites and screen printing	Basic screen printing techniques to transfer designs onto the kite	New		120 minutes	**	Themed scarves, Character hotels, Kite bonanza
LIRT 5 Protection: quilted skating mitts	To produce a padded fabric by quilting	New		120 minutes	**	Travel safe
LIRT 6 Street style: T-shirt and baseball cap decoration	To decorate with transfer printing and spray painting	New		120 minutes	**	Customized carriers, Feely bags unlimited, Character hotels
LIRT 7 Tents: investigating seams, reinforcements and loops	To practise seams, machine sewing, testing and evaluating; to make and test reinforcements and loops	Recap and extension	Science	Part 1: 60 minutes Part 2: 60 minutes	**	Customized carriers, Happy cotton, Squashy seats, Snuggly buggly
LIRT 8 The theatre: costumes for a dance routine	To use darts to achieve 3D textile forms	New		120 minutes	***	A cast of thousands, Audition kit bag
PART 1 Investigating a single product	To extend understanding of how to investigate products	Recap and extension		80 minutes	*	Can be used with any Capability Tasks as appropriate
PART 2 Investigating a collection of products	To extend understanding of how to investigate products	Recap and extension		80 minutes	**	Can be used with any Capability Tasks as appropriate

Part 2

Capability Tasks for 14–16 year-olds

Capability Task Summary Tables

© The Nuffield Foundation, 1996

Line of interest	Task title	Nature of product	Useful Resource Tasks	Useful Case Studies
Fashion accessories	Home comforts	Slip-on felt shoes, unisex in appeal; rag boots; woven cosmic footsies; baby Eco-slips; Viking long boots for those dark winter evenings!; patchwork pop socks	SRT 2 Questionnaires SRT 4 Brainstorming CRT 4 Capturing fabric on paper CRT 6 Communicating to the maker LIRT 4 Accessories – weaving a small bag (this can be restricted to recycled fabrics)	Clothing manufacture, Colour and colourways
Fashion accessories	Themed scarves	A range of shapes of scarves; a cut-out figure showing 'scarf' being worn several different ways; a sample board of pattern exploration; 4 scarves to show 'Themed Dicams' potential range in providing promotional products that have sufficient style to become part of extended product ranges	SRT 5 Attribute analysis CRT 1 Mood boards and theme boards DRT 2 Batik snowflakes MFRT 1 Rally arm band LIRT 2 Kites and screen printing LIRT 7 Bags and carriers – simple bag decorated with block printing	Corporate clothing
Bags and carriers	Customized carriers	An advertisement linked to a small display, all photographed for a marketing flyer that offers to customize carriers for cars; a range of flat-packed (bagged) carriers for sale at trolley pick-up point or on entering a supermarket	CRT 1 Mood boards and theme boards CRT 4 Capturing fabric on paper CRT 6 Communicating to the maker LIRT 1 Tents – investigating seams, reinforcements and loops LIRT 7 Bags and carriers – simple bag decorated with block printing	Bags and carriers, Corporate clothing
Bags and carriers	Feely bags unlimited	An 'egg-box' containing six bags made of different texture fabrics, each fastened and finished differently and each containing a different pebble. Inside the lid is a suggested script for the teacher/parent; a 'shoe-box' containing small draw-string bags each made of different fabrics – they contain a card on which is written what the fabric is commonly used for. For example non-woven fabric – dish-cloths	SRT 1 Identifying needs and likes SRT 4 Brainstorming SRT 5 Attribute analysis CRT 4 How to capture fabric on paper CRT 6 Communicating to the maker FCRT 2 Knitting to make textured buttons	A textile designer's story
Interiors	Character hotels	Either Presentation sheets of themed fabric samples showing where designs could be applied; lengths of fabric, to scale, for use as certain material; lampshades and napkins showing designs Or One-off piece made to a high standard with a presentation sheet indicating its relationship to the overall theme	CRT 1 Mood boards and theme boards CRT 4 Capturing fabric on paper CRT 5 Exploring interiors DRT 1 Tie and dye with natural dyes DRT 2 Batik snowflakes FCRT 1 Layering LIRT 2 Kites and screen printing LIRT 6 Interiors – wall hanging for a child's bedroom LIRT 7 Bags and carriers – simple bag decorated with block printing	A textile designer's story, Colour and colourways

Capability Task Summary Tables

Line of Interest	Task title	Nature of product	Useful Resource Tasks	Useful Case Studies
Interiors	Squashy seats	Giant cup and saucer bags; tomato pouffes; chess floor cushions; baked-bean bags; Godzilla bag; the Shushion – for that quiet moment in your life; huggy cushion; fantastic floor furniture; bum cushion	SRT 1 Needs and likes SRT 2 Questionnaires SRT 4 Brainstorming SRT 5 Attribute analysis FCRT 3 Investigating the structure of fabrics LIRT 1 Tents – investigating seams, reinforcements and loops	A textile designer's story
Kites	Kite bonanza	Humming pie kite; angel cake kite; muffin marvel; fairy flyer; stunning sandwich cake; cherry charmer; baklava blower	CRT 1 Mood boards and theme boards CRT 4 Capturing fabric on paper CRT 6 Communicating to the maker LIRT 2 Kites and screen printing DRT 2 Batik snowflakes	Corporate clothing
Protection	Clean cuisine	A prototype uniform to be tested for use. This may include: cap, net, hat, waistcoat cum apron, trousers, wrap-around coverall, clogs; a simple model of the food outlet, showing how the protective clothing complements/ enhances the Food Fare Inc. corporate image	SRT 2 Questionnaires SRT 5 Attribute analysis CRT 3 Fashion drawing FCRT 3 Investigating the structure of fabrics	Corporate clothing
Protection	Travel safe	Visible 'bibs'; fun exterior belts and braces; elbow reflectors; knee pads; hand flashes; helmet stretch nets; jacket patches	SRT 1 Identifying needs and likes SRT 4 Brainstorming CRT 4 How to capture fabric on paper CRT 6 Communicating to the maker LIRT 5 Protection – quilted skating mitts	Protective clothing, Clothing manufacture

© The Nuffield Foundation, 1996

Capability Task Summary Tables

Line of interest	Task title	Nature of product	Useful Resource Tasks	Useful Case Studies
Street style	Happy cotton	T-shirts with printed images/slogans such as 'Happy Cotton Bud' © 'Cotton-u-like' 'Cotton on – it's OK' 'Cool Cotton – does no harm' plus a zigzag storyboard and an image board for T-shirts as part of a display	SRT 1 Identifying needs and likes SRT 2 Questionnaires CRT 1 Mood boards and theme boards CRT 2 Presenting data LIRT 1 Kites and screen printing LIRT 7 Bags and carriers – simple bag decorated with block printing	Saidpur women textile group Bangladesh
Street style	Rap wrap	Animal wrap; wild wrap; sports gown; dressing-up gown; champion wrap; all with applied decorative detail to illustrate themes	CRT 1 Mood boards and theme boards CRT 3 Fashion drawing CRT 6 Communicating to the maker LIRT 6 Interiors – a wall hanging for a child's bedroom	Design at Dorothy Perkins, New fashion textiles
Tents	Snuggly buggly	Building block bungalows; tepees for tots; liquorice alsorts houses; sweet dreams – all constructed from strong fabric, stiffened with 'ribs'	SRT 1 Identifying needs and likes SRT 4 Brainstorming SRT 5 Attribute analysis CRT 4 How to capture fabric on paper CRT 6 Communicating to the maker LIRT 1 Tents: investigating seams, reinforcements and loops	Tents
The theatre	A cast of thousands	T-shaped black garment; waistcoat; tabard; cloak/wrap; range of accessories to convert simple garment to costume for each of the productions	CRT 1 Mood boards and theme boards CRT 2 Presenting data CRT 3 Fashion drawing CRT 6 Communicating to the maker LIRT 3 Costumes for a dance routine	Design at Dorothy Perkins
The theatre	Audition kit bag	hat; crown; armour; cloak; mask; bow tie; scarf; pinafore; sash	SRT 1 Identifying needs and likes CRT 1 Mood boards and theme boards CRT 3 Fashion drawing CRT 6 Communicating to the maker LIRT 3 Costumes for a dance routine	Design at Dorothy Perkins

© The Nuffield Foundation, 1996

Home comforts 1

A Capability Task for textiles
Line of interest – fashion accessories

The task

To design and make a pair of indoor shoes/slippers that use reclaimed or reused materials in their construction.

Task setting

Indoor shoes, slippers, moccasins – none of them sounds very inspiring. They seem to have appeal for the very young or the very old. With the present-day concern for environmental issues, Green Feet Ltd have set themselves up as producers of Eco-slips – indoor shoes made entirely from reclaimed textiles. They are keen that their Eco-slips are as up to date as possible. They see their target audience as students and interested young adults. Part of their work is the development of new applications for old techniques with reclaimed textiles, so they would like some ideas for a whole range with broad appeal.

The aims of the task

- to enable students to gather data for market research
- to teach the communication techniques needed to describe the overall form, parts and assembly of a product
- to enable students to select materials using a wide range of criteria and develop high-quality making skills
- to enable students to consider designing and making for manufacture when reviewing the feasibility of their product.

Values

technical
Students should consider the properties required by slipper fabric and whether this can be achieved with reused textiles.

economic
Students should consider the real cost of using apparently cheap raw materials, e.g. sourcing, cleaning, labour, etc.

aesthetic
Students should examine a range of 'best-selling slippers' and look for common themes.

moral
Students should consider the argument that we are stewards of the world and have an obligation to protect it for future inhabitants.

social
Students should consider how, where, when and by whom slippers are worn.

environmental
Students should prepare a comparative study of two similar products: one from reused materials, one not (tissues for example).

Nature of the product

from exploration
The students should produce:
- a report on 'the slipper-wearing habits' of a particular target group, e.g. class
- a report on a range of slippers currently available which looks in detail at:
  – the customer
  – the style
  – the materials used
  – the cost
- a report on two methods of reusing textiles, e.g. felt and rags
- a preliminary specification for a new product.

for the production and promotion
The students should produce:
- a selection of ideas to be evaluated against the product specification
- a detailed specification for final products including textiles, how reused, equipment, cost and production schedule
- samples of reuse of textiles
- ideas for the launch of the Eco-slip.

possible products
- slip-on felt shoes, unisex in appeal
- rag boots
- woven cosmic footsies
- baby Eco-slips
- Viking long boots for those dark winter evenings!
- patchwork pop socks.

Some students may wish to consider the packaging of their product.

Technical knowledge and understanding

- knowledge of textile properties
- knowledge of recycling techniques
- knowledge of slipper-making techniques
- knowledge of manufacturing techniques in the shoe industry.

Specialist tools, materials and equipment

- a range of slippers to be disassembled
- a range of reclaimed textile products – rag rugs, patchwork
- industrial sewing machine
- overlocker.

Cross-curricular links

maths
- measuring and fitting 3D shapes, e.g. feet to explore the limits of too big and too small.

science
- an exploration of the factors affecting useful life of different fabrics; how long can it go on?

art
- ways of simplifying complex natural forms such as feet for illustration purposes.

IT
- use of CAD software to draw networks for packaging; use of DTP software to produce packaging copy.

economic and industrial understanding
- the role and place of craft-based industry and how this may develop in the context of companies concerned with eco-products.

Useful Resource Tasks

To enable students to gather data for market research:
- SRT 2 *Questionnaires*.

To teach the communication techniques needed to describe the overall form, parts and assembly of a product:
- CRT 4 *Capturing fabric on paper*
- CRT 6 *Communicating to the maker*.

To enable students to select materials using a wide range of criteria and develop high-quality making skills:
- SRT 4 *Brainstorming*
- LIRT 1 *Fashion accessories – weaving a small bag* (this can be restricted to recycled fabrics).

Useful Case Studies

To enable students to consider designing and making for manufacture when reviewing the feasibility of their product:

'Clothing manufacture' (*Student's Book*, page 70),
'Colour and colourways' (*Student's Book*, page 68).

Design brief

To design and make a pair of wearable indoor shoes from reclaimed textiles. Prepare a possible production schedule indicating how batch production could be achieved.

Specification

What the product should do:
- be made from reclaimed textiles
- be suitable for indoor shoe wear
- demonstrate innovation in use of techniques.

What the product should look like:
- an elegant eco-shoe, or a funny eco-shoe!

Other features:
- suitable for a particular retail outlet
- appropriate eco-friendly box packaging.

Possible associated activities

- visit retail outlet and make observations on present ranges of slippers/indoor shoes
- arrange visit/talk from shoe manufacturer or retailer
- research current eco-products, especially textile-based ones.

Design sketches

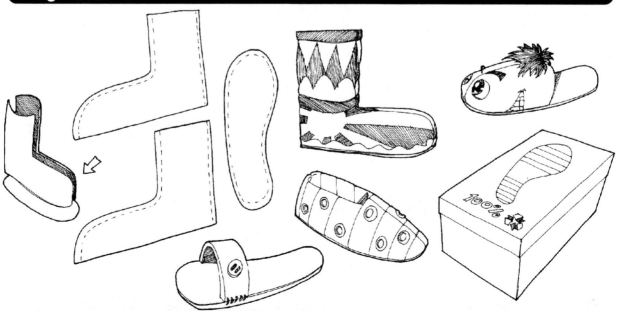

Information for making

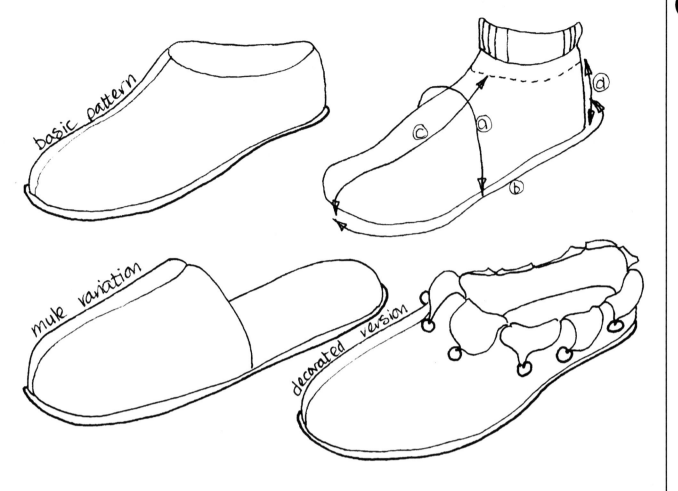

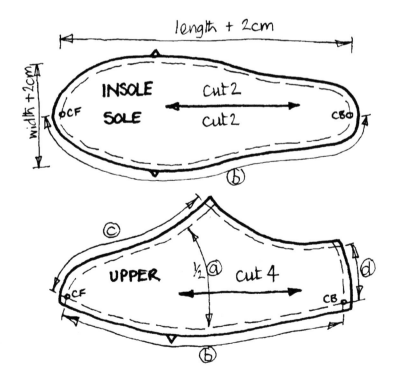

Will slipper fit over widest part of foot?

Will upper need to be made from stretch fabric?

Is it better to use binding for top edge, use a facing or add a lining to upper?

How can the sole be made non-slip?

Resources
- edging for top
- stiffening for sole

1 Home comforts

2 Themed scarves

A Capability Task for textiles
Line of interest – fashion accessories

The task
To design and make a decorated scarf that promotes products.

Task setting
Themed Events are a textile company who specialize in designing and making promotional textile products, particularly scarves for events such as launching a new book or the opening of a new resource. London Zoo have recently opened a new nocturnal house. To launch the house they plan to invite guests to an evening event and as part of the invitation they are including a scarf to be worn on the night. The zoo needs designs for the decoration, fabric and shape of the scarf and it needs to appeal to both men and women.

The aims of the task
- to enable students to use an analysis of an organization to inform their designing and making
- to enable students to investigate and analyse a range of existing products, e.g. scarves, and their potential for use in a large-scale promotion
- to enable students to develop high-quality fabric decoration techniques
- to enable students to consider batch production of textiles in terms of cost, ease of manufacture and finish.

Values

technical
Students should consider production techniques suitable for high-quality outcomes.

economic
Students should consider the costs and benefits of promotional goods.

aesthetic
Students should consider what designs could have general appeal. Should they be safe or outrageous?

moral
Students should consider whether 'the ends', that is to say more people attending and enjoying an event to promote something, justifies 'the means' – the give-away textile item.

social
Students should consider the place of promotion in terms of how a successful promotion can lead to the success of the event.

environmental
Students should consider the chemical composition of the printing inks/dyes used in terms of their disposability.

Nature of the product

from exploration
The students should produce:
- a report on typical promotional products in the supermarket/in magazines
- a report on scarves – who wears them, how, when and where
- an investigation in terms of cost, availability and suitability of a range of fabrics
- a suggestion sheet of how people wear scarves
- exploration of a range of techniques for finished effect, such as batik, screen printing, block printing
- a preliminary specification for a new textile product plus how it would be packaged as part of a promotion.

for the production and promotion
The students should produce:
- a selection of textile product ideas which are evaluated against the product specification
- a detailed specification for final products which includes materials, equipment and production schedule
- an image board of the potential client group
- a presentation board of ideas for the client
- a linked invitation card 'How will you wear this tarantula scarf when you attend the Nocturnal House Nosh?'

possible products
- a range of shapes of scarves
- a cut-out figure showing 'scarf' being worn several different ways
- a sample board of pattern exploration
- four scarves to show 'Themed Events' potential range in providing promotional products that have sufficient style to become part of extended product ranges.

Technical knowledge and understanding
- knowledge of decoration techniques
- knowledge of edge finishing methods
- knowledge of handling delicate fabrics
- knowledge of batch production.

Specialist tools, materials and equipment

- access to photocopier for repeat pattern work
- access to magazines with animal photographs
- access to CD-ROM with animal images.

Cross-curricular links

maths
- repeated pattern, tessellation; calculating how many scarves per metre.

science
- investigation into keeping qualities of decoration techniques given wear and care.

art
- patterns from natural and man-made sources.

IT
- use of CAD/CAM to produce stencils and blocks; use of CAD to produce networks for packaging; use of DTP software for production of invitation card.

economic and industrial understanding
- importance of promotion as marketing tool.

Useful Resource Tasks

To enable students to investigate and analyse a range of existing products, e.g. scarves, and their potential for use in a large-scale promotion:
- SRT 5 *Attribute analysis*
- CRT 1 *Mood boards and theme boards*.

To enable students to develop high-quality fabric decoration techniques:
- DRT 2 *Batik snowflakes*
- LIRT 2 *Bags and carriers – simple bag decorated with block printing*
- LIRT 4 *Kites and screen printing*.

To enable students to consider batch production of textiles in terms of cost, ease of manufacture and finish:
- MfRT 1 *Rally arm band*.

Useful Case Studies

To enable students to use an analysis of an organization to inform their designing and making:
'Corporate clothing' (*Student's Book*, page 48).

Design brief

To design and make a range of decorated scarves that:
- can be used as part of a promotional event
- can be worn by males and females alike
- reflects the theme strongly.

Specification

What the product should do:
- promote London Zoo (or similar).

What the product should look like:
- use animals as a decorative theme in a distinctive and stylish manner.

Other features:
- be attractive to both men and women
- be available from the zoo or by mail order
- have attractive packaging which includes suggestions for wear.

Possible associated activities

- visit two or three stores to examine range of scarves
- detailed observation for one hour in busy street noting down incidence of scarves worn
- brainstorming ways of wearing a scarf
- presentation sheets showing, for example: from owl to turban; from monkey to muffler; from snake to silky wrap.

Design sketches

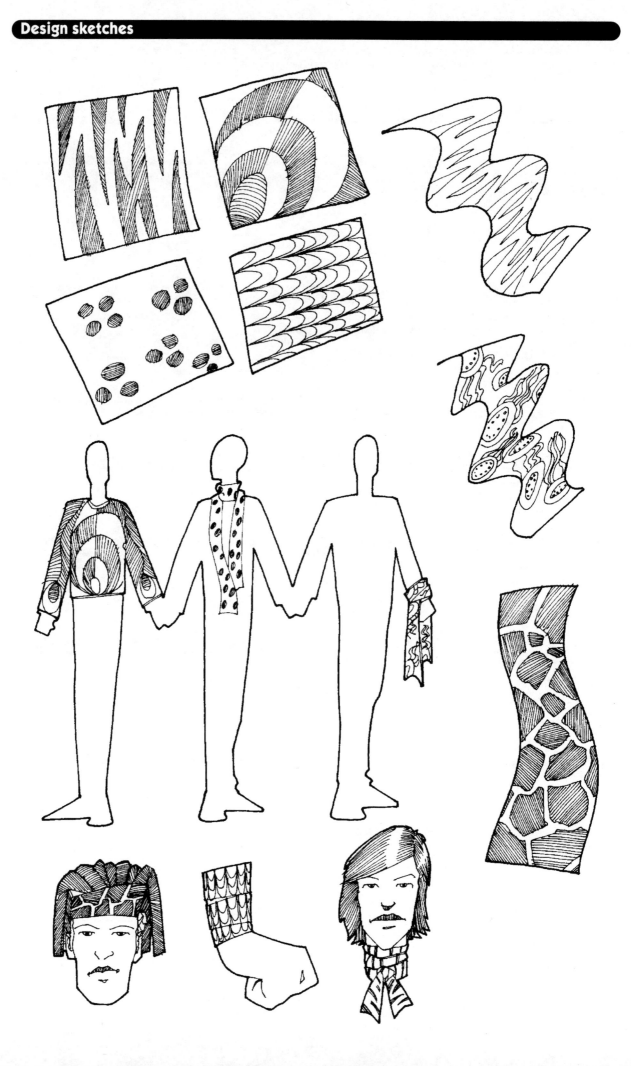

Information for making

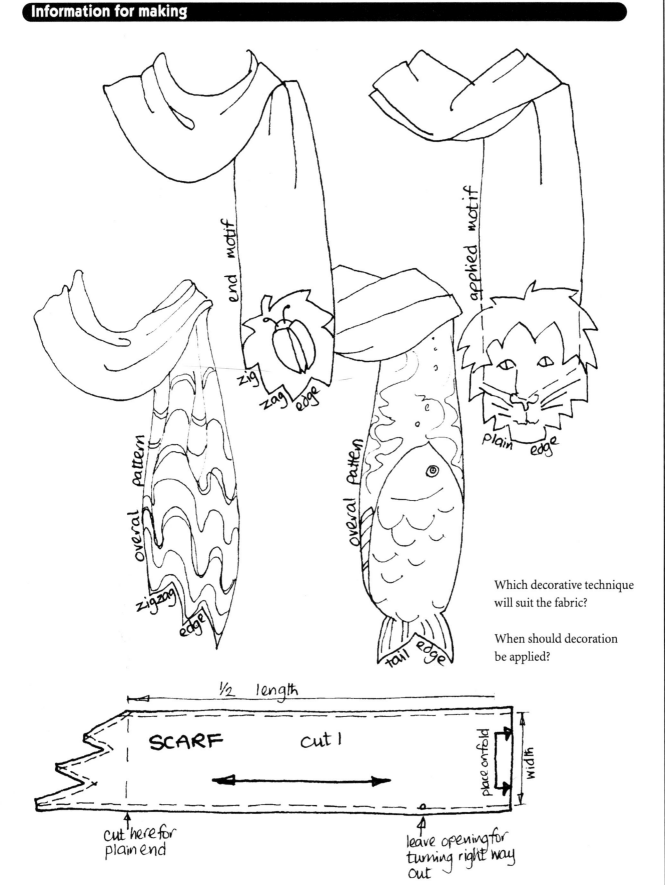

Which decorative technique will suit the fabric?

When should decoration be applied?

2 Themed scarves

3 Customized carriers

A Capability Task for textiles
Line of interest – bags and carriers

The task
To design and make to prototype stage a range of customized bags/carriers that fit rigid containers.

Task setting
Many people find the use of boxes and plastic bags at the check-outs in supermarkets a frustrating experience. Even if there is a packer the goods have to be transferred from trolley to car boot and car boot to home – often a tedious chore. Tex-Ends Ltd are a small family firm who specialize in textile products from other manufacturers' offcuts. They would like to diversify and produce bags and carriers. They have purchased 10,000 metres of strong calico and need a product range and a good marketing angle. They have decided to develop supermarket trolley bags.

The aims of the task
- to teach the communication techniques needed to describe the overall form, parts and assembly of a product
- to develop an understanding of imagery used in promotion
- to enable students to develop high-quality making skills needed for a robust product
- to develop skills in simple decoration techniques.

Values

technical
Students should consider how seams can be made strong.

economic
Students should consider the risk of launching innovative products on the market. How will the initial investment be recouped?

aesthetic
Students should consider if these products need to be functional or funky!

moral
Students should consider whether a company is right to promote more consumption through its marketing strategy.

social
Students should consider modern lifestyles and the need for bags/carriers that serve this specific purpose.

environmental
Students should consider the production of calico cloth and its impact on the environment.

Nature of the product

from exploration
The students should produce:
- an analysis of existing textile carriers, their use and their possible development
- an exploration of possible 'sites' for customized carriers, for example car boots, supermarket trolleys, suitcases, tool boxes, toilet bags, toy boxes
- a range of shapes modelled from calico to assess ease of cut, join and finish
- a preliminary specification for a new product.

for the production and promotion
The students should produce:
- a selection of product ideas that are evaluated against the product specification
- a detailed specification for final production that includes equipment, materials and production schedule
- a sample board of possible finishes for the calico, for example letters stencilled, printing, contrast piping, binding
- a small range of miniature samples made from paper.

possible products
- an advertisement linked to a small display, all photographed for a marketing flyer that offers to customize carriers for cars
- a range of flat-packed (bagged) carriers for sale at trolley pick-up points or on entering a supermarket.

Technical knowledge and understanding
- knowledge of fabric testing
- knowledge and understanding of pattern cutting
- knowledge and understanding of joining and finishing seams and edges
- knowledge of fabric printing techniques.

Specialist tools, materials and equipment
- different samples of calico-type fabric
- access to supermarket trolleys.

Cross-curricular links

maths
- accurate measurement, calculating volume, knowledge of 3D cuboid shapes.

science
- investigation into likely loads in shopping trolleys and loads that can be easily lifted from trolleys to car boots.

art
- analysis of the supermarket image and its potential for a bag decoration.

IT
- use of CAD/CAM to generate networks for small paper models; use of CAD/CAM to generate printing blocks.

economic and industrial understanding
- consideration of the factors affecting the price of the product in terms of both manufacturing costs and what consumers will pay for such an item.

Useful Resource Tasks

To develop an understanding of imagery used in promotional work:
- CRT 1 *Mood boards and theme boards.*

To teach the communication techniques needed to describe the overall form, parts and assembly of a product:
- CRT 4 *Capturing fabric on paper*
- CRT 6 *Communicating to the maker.*

To enable students to develop high-quality making skills needed for a robust product:
- LIRT 1 *Tents – investigating seams, reinforcements and loops.*

To develop skills in simple decoration techniques:
- LIRT 2 *Bags and carriers – simple bag decorated with block printing.*

Useful Case Studies

To develop an understanding of imagery used in promotion:
'Bags and carriers' (*Student's Book*, page 46),
'Corporate clothing' (*Student's Book*, page 48).

Design brief

To design and make a textile carrier that can fit into a car boot or supermarket trolley and then be easily transferred to a car or home.

Specification

What the product should do:
- serve as a useful lining for a rigid container
- carry loads associated with shopping
- be reusable many times.

What the product should look like:
- promote a retail outlet
- have a natural finish and feel.

Other features:
- be manufactured from calico
- be able to be flat-packed and sold hanging up.

Possible associated activities

- visit supermarket to record difficulties and problems with packing and transporting goods
- visit textile production factory
- brainstorm of 'Why not just plastic bags forever?'

Design sketches

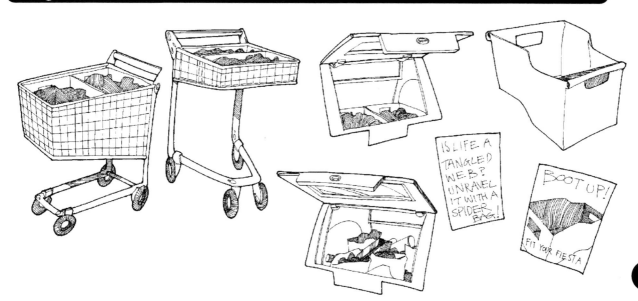

Information for making

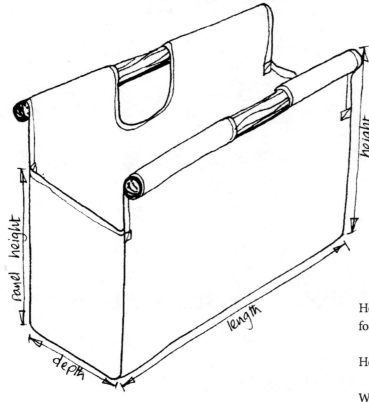

How can you check the strength of your bag, for the load it is designed to carry?

How will the handle be kept in place?

What is the best way of edging openings?

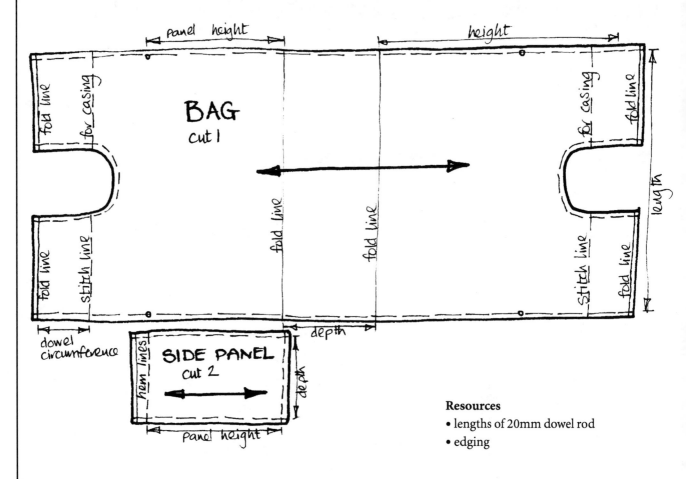

Resources
- lengths of 20mm dowel rod
- edging

Feely bags unlimited 4

A Capability Task for textiles
Line of interest – bags and carriers

The task
To design and make a set of feely bags for use as an educational/developmental aid.

Task setting
Brita Toys are a toy company with a difference – they deal exclusively with institutions who need speech aids. Typical of their clients is a speech unit attached to a nursery school or a stroke rehabilitation centre. Their latest idea is a set of surprising feely bags that both look and feel interesting and contain something that intrigues. Their function is to encourage speech. The bags are really to promote questions and answers. The company is anxious to trial its idea and needs prototypes developed.

The aims of the task
- to enable students to design for a particular age group
- to teach the communication techniques needed to describe the parts, action and assembly of a product
- to enable students to select materials using a wide range of criteria and develop high-quality making skills.

Values

technical
Students should consider how openings can be made interesting and challenging yet not daunting.

economic
Students should consider factors affecting the price and quality of products produced for low-volume markets.

aesthetic
Students should consider what makes an attractive bag. How can a set be the same yet different?

moral
Students should consider their responsibility towards disadvantaged groups.

social
Students should consider the development or redevelopment of speech.

environmental
Students should consider how recycled materials might be used in their products.

Nature of the product

from exploration
The students should produce:
- a report on a range of educational toys either from direct observation or from catalogues
- a report on nursery children's normal development of speech
- ideas sheet of bag designs and contents; size, shape, finish
- ideas for compartmentalized structure to contain the bags
- a preliminary for a new product.

for the production and promotion
The students should produce:
- a selection of product ideas that are evaluated against the product specification
- a detailed specification for final products including materials, equipment and production schedule
- a report on 'what grabs a three year old' – possible lines of interest based on observation and reading.

possible products
- an 'egg-box' containing six bags made of different texture fabrics, each fastened and finished differently and each containing a different pebble. Inside the lid is a suggested script for the teacher/parent
- a 'shoe-box' containing small draw-string bags each made of different fabrics – they contain a card on which is written what the fabric is commonly used for, for example non-woven fabric – dishcloths.

Technical knowledge and understanding
- knowledge of range of textiles and their properties and qualities
- knowledge of methods of fastening, joining fabric.

Specialist tools, materials and equipment
- wide range of textile samples
- eyelet maker
- wide range of fastenings
- range of children's/adults' magazines/books
- educational suppliers' catalogues.

Cross-curricular links

maths
- anthropometric investigations into variation in hand size and the shape/volume of bag needed to provide for adequate 'feeling'.

science
- an investigation of the properties required by fabrics to be used in feely bags for 3 year olds.

art
- looking with touch rather than eyes!

IT
- using DTP software to produce sample scripts.

economic and industrial understanding
- the place of specialist products in the marketplace.

English
- developing an appropriate script for use with the feely bags.

Useful Resource Tasks

To enable students to design for a particular age group:
- SRT 1 *Identifying needs and likes*.

To teach the communication techniques needed to describe the parts, action and assembly of a product:
- CRT 4 *How to capture fabric on paper*
- CRT 6 *Communicating to the maker*.

To enable students to select materials using a wide range of criteria and develop high-quality making skills:
- SRT 4 *Brainstorming*
- SRT 5 *Attribute analysis*
- FCRT 2 *Knitting to make textured buttons*.

Useful Case Studies

To enable students to select materials using a wide range of criteria:
'A textile designer's story' (*Student's Book*, page 42).

Design brief

To design and make a set of textile feely bags that will act as a speech prompt. They must each be different in feel and fastening and must be housed in a rigid container with a sample script to promote speech.

Specification

What the product should do:
- act as a prompt for speech.

What the product should look like:
- be in the form of a small bag(s)
- be attractive, irresistible to fingers!
- be intriguing and puzzling.

Other features:
- be based on a range of textiles
- show different fastening techniques
- be compact and portable.

Possible associated activities

- a talk from a speech therapist or occupational therapist on encouraging speech
- visit to nursery or nursery special unit to observe children
- brainstorming of possible bag contents
- trial of scripts in pairs.

Design sketches

Information for making

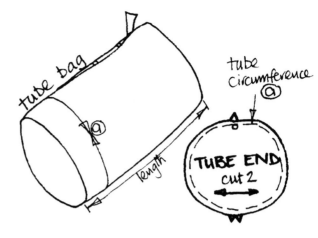
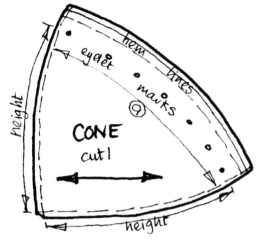
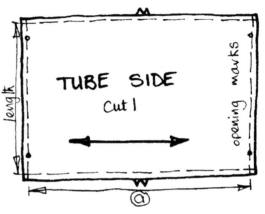
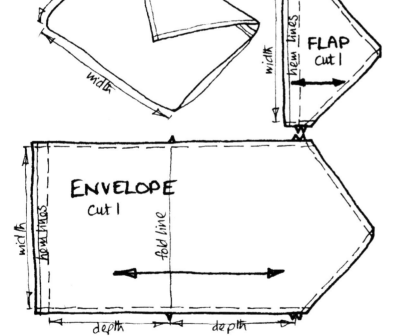

How will you choose fabrics to suit the bag shape?

How will the fabric affect the way you make the bag?

What size would be best?

What fastening would be most suitable?

Resources
- fastenings
- stiffenings (possible)

5 Character hotels

A Capability Task for textiles
Line of interest – interiors

The task
To design and make to a range of decorative textiles to be used in commercial situations.

Task setting
Walk into any hotel and you expect a feeling of comfort and luxury from the interior. Hotels often use textile products for this and also to carry their logo. All hotel products are normally part of the corporate identity, from the complimentary soap in the bathroom to the cover of the menu. New hotels or refurbished hotels therefore call in textile consultants to develop their whole image. One new venture is a chain of hotels based on the coast around Great Britain. Each hotel has a particular character which the hotel chain, Seaspray Ltd, want to preserve. However, they would like their name to be reflected in the interior design. They would like a range of themed textile designs for their hotels. Some of them are named below:
- Far Lighthouse Hotel (10 beds)
- Gull and Herring Hotel (20 beds)
- Calm Waters Hotel (100 beds)
- Safe Harbour Hotel (10 beds).

The aims of the task
- to enable students to explore and present interior design ideas
- to enable students to consider decorative techniques for batch-produced decorative textile products
- to enable students to consider decorative techniques for one-off textile products
- to enable students to consider the commercial production of textiles.

Values

technical
Students should consider how craft-based approaches to decorating fabrics change when a manufacturing process is involved.

economic
Students should consider the overall cost implications of heavily patterned, multi-coloured designs, and how much can be charged for the 'added value' of coordinated design in hotels.

aesthetic
Students should consider the possibility of producing kitsch when responding to a theme.

moral
Students should consider the worth of costly theme design based refurbishment.

social
Students should consider general public taste rather than their own.

environmental
Students should consider the role of design in providing energy efficiency in the running of a hotel.

Nature of the product

from exploration
Students should produce:
- a study of the fabric designs in the school, with a map of where they are located
- a similar study of a local hotel
- an image board for the hotel
- initial rough sketches of ideas for design
- presentation sheets plus fabric samples with lists of possible applications for designs
- a preliminary specification of two sorts of product:
  – a one-off commission, e.g. appliqué wall hanging, layered construction
  – a batch produced item, e.g. curtains, napkin corners, lampshade edges.

for the production and promotion
The students should produce:
- a selection of product ideas which are evaluated against the product specification
- a detailed specification for the final product ideas including fabric, designs, method of printing, methods of construction, production schedule, cost, and more general application of the design throughout the hotel
- printed samples pack (paper only) to be used to inform the client.

possible products
Either
- presentation sheets of themed fabric samples showing where designs could be applied
- lengths of fabric, to scale, for use as curtain material
- lampshades and napkins showing designs.

Or
- one-off piece made to a high standard with a presentation sheet indicating its relationship to the overall theme
- goods for sale in hotel souvenir shop.

Technical knowledge and understanding
- knowledge of printing techniques
- knowledge of construction techniques.

Specialist tools, materials and equipment

- photocopier for repeat pattern work.

Cross-curricular links

maths
- scaling-up techniques; the cost of 1 metre of printed fabric and 1000 metres; estimating and measuring large areas.

science
- investigating the keeping qualities of decorated fabrics given wear and care.

art
- use of observational drawing to develop design ideas based on a theme.

IT
- use of CAD/CAM to produce printing blocks; use of CAD/CAM to produce embroidery based decoration; use of CAD/CAM to produce decorative knitted panels.

economic and industrial understanding
- consideration of the cost and benefits of refurbishment.

Useful Resource Tasks

To enable students to explore and present interior design ideas:
- CRT 1 *Mood boards and theme boards*
- CRT 4 *Capturing fabric on paper*
- CRT 5 *Exploring interiors.*

To enable students to consider decorative techniques for batch-produced decorative textile products:
- LIRT 2 *Bags and carriers – simple bag decorated with block printing*
- LIRT 4 *Kites and screen printing.*

To enable students to consider decorative techniques for one-off textile products:
- FCRT 1 *Layering*
- DRT 1 *Tie-dyeing with natural dyes*
- DRT 2 *Batik snowflakes*
- LIRT 3 *Interiors – wall hanging for a child's bedroom.*

Useful Case Studies

To enable students to consider the commercial production of textiles:
'A textile designer's story' (*Student's Book*, page 42),
'Colour and colourways' (*Student's Book*, page 68).

Design brief

To develop the interior design of a hotel from a theme. To design and make a new range of printed textiles that support the theme of the hotel. To design and make a one-off piece made to a high standard in keeping with the overall theme of the hotel.

Specification

printed textiles

What the product(s) should do:
- provide decoration on a variety of items in keeping with the theme of the hotel.

What the product(s) should look like:
- reflect the theme and the hotel group image
- be presented as part of a complete range.

Other features:
- be durable
- maintain quality appearance given wear and care.

one-off piece

What the product should do:
- provide additional visual attraction to the interior.

What the product should look like:
- be based on the hotel theme
- be in tune with the appearance, style and ambience of the interior.

Other features:
- be safe in terms of fixtures and fitting
- be easily maintained
- be easily cleaned.

Possible associated activities

- visit textile factory
- visit furnishing fabric department of local department store
- visit from the buyer from the textile department to talk about considerations
- interview local hotel manager – what would they look for in designs for a hotel?
- brainstorm of images that reflect names.

Design sketches

Information for making

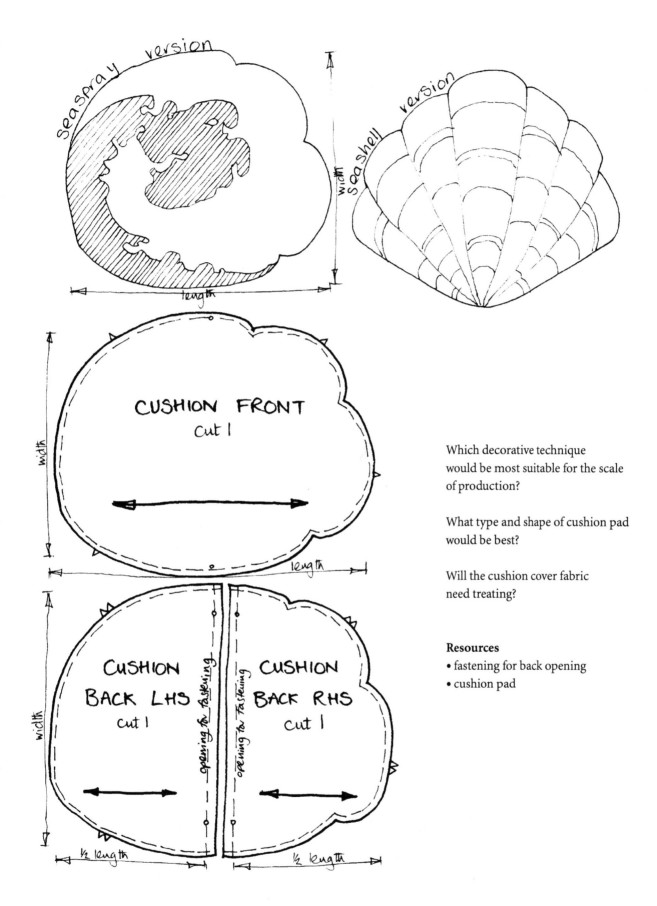

Which decorative technique would be most suitable for the scale of production?

What type and shape of cushion pad would be best?

Will the cushion cover fabric need treating?

Resources
- fastening for back opening
- cushion pad

6 Squashy seats

A Capability Task for textiles
Line of interest – interiors

The task
To design and make a bean bag type seat that is aimed at a particular market.

Task setting
Bags to sit on have been around for about twenty years. They are usually sold for children's rooms. Have you ever sat on one? Seating Unlimited is a small company who have been producing Green Bean Bags for several years and are anxious to develop the product range. Your task is to design an innovative, attractive bean bag type seat, give it a name and suggest where it might be sold.

The aims of the task
- to enable students to develop high-quality making skills needed for a robust product
- to enable students to investigate designing for a retail outlet and the role of customer preference
- to enable students to think about extending a range of products
- to enable students to consider fabric choice for a robust product.

Values

technical
Students should consider the following issues – strength of seams, durability of covering and stuffing, safety aspects.

economic
Students should consider the cost of this form of seating compared to another.

aesthetic
Students should consider how to make a squashy fat bag on the floor look appealing in the marketplace.

moral
Students should take into account the possible sensitive nature of any visual jokes they build into their bag seats.

social
Students should consider the wider use and application of this form of seating, for example with the handicapped.

environmental
Students should consider the source of the materials they choose and their potential for reuse and recycling before disposal.

Nature of the product

from exploration
The students should produce:
- a report on different seating styles, considering different times and cultures
- a report on existing products, including price range, customer profile and range
- an image board of 'who sits on the floor?'
- a preliminary specification for a new product
- a short case study of bean bags made for pets – from a personal point of view – based on store visits, plus some research through reading.

for the production and promotion
The students should produce:
- a selection of product ideas which are evaluated against the product specification
- a detailed specification for the final product including materials, equipment, costs involved, production schedule and possible retail outlets
- a collection of images that could be used as an advertisement on a billboard or in a magazine.

possible products
- giant cup and saucer bags
- tomato pouffes
- chess floor cushions
- baked-bean bags
- Godzilla bag
- the Shushion – for that quiet moment in your life
- huggy cushion
- fantastic floor furniture
- bum cushion.

Technical knowledge and understanding
- knowledge and understanding of construction techniques for heavy-duty fabrics
- knowledge and understanding of the properties and qualities of covering and stuffing materials.

Specialist tools, materials and equipment
- range of heavy-duty textiles to compare, test and evaluate for suitability
- range of stuffing materials to compare, test and evaluate with particular regard for safety
- illustrations of range of seating options with reference to other times and other cultures
- range of fastenings to explore.

Cross-curricular links

maths
- area – calculating how much covering is needed; volume – calculating how much filling is needed.

science
- investigation into durability of materials.

art
- using observational drawing as a basis for developing ideas for enhancing a shapeless seat!

IT
- using CAD/CAM to explore colourways on design ideas.

economic and industrial understanding
- costing of materials to produce 10 000 seats; calculating the warehouse storage needed for 10 000 seats.

Useful Resource Tasks

To enable students to develop high-quality making skills needed for a robust product:
- LIRT 7 *Tents – investigating seams, reinforcements and loops.*

To enable students to investigate designing for a retail outlet and the role of customer preference:
- SRT 1 *Needs and likes*
- SRT 2 *Questionnaires.*

To enable students to think about extending a range of products:
- SRT 4 *Brainstorming*
- SRT 5 *Attribute analysis.*

To enable students to consider fabric choice for a robust product:
- FCRT 3 *Investigating the structure of fabrics.*

Useful Case Studies

To enable students to consider fabric choice for a robust product:
'A textile designer's story' (*Student's Book*, page 42).

Design brief

To design and make a textile seat based on the bean bag principle and on an innovative idea and repositions bean bags in the market!

Specification

What the product should do:
- provide an alternative comfortable solution to sitting on the floor!

What the product should look like:
- attractive and safe
- linked to an identifiable theme.

Other features:
- sturdy and well made
- be safe and secure as a piece of furniture.

Possible associated activities

- visit local store to look at range of seating available
- focus study on bean bag availability
- research into who would use a bean bag
- brainstorm of new product ideas
- collection of product catalogues
- collection of anthropometric data.

Design sketches

Information for making

Squashy seats 6

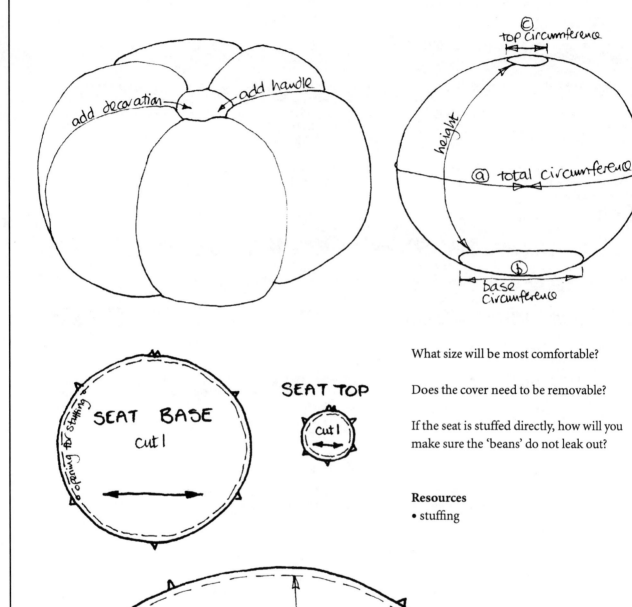

What size will be most comfortable?

Does the cover need to be removable?

If the seat is stuffed directly, how will you make sure the 'beans' do not leak out?

Resources
- stuffing

Kite bonanza 7

A Capability Task for textiles
Line of interest – kites

The task

To design and make a kite suitable to be flown during a town's 'kite bonanza'.

Task setting

The kite bonanza is sponsored by Fairy Airy Cakes Ltd, who produce a range of boxed cakes and whose slogan is 'Cakes that float in the mouth, cakes as light as air'. Fairy Airy Cakes would like the kites to reflect the products, either in shape, decoration or applied graphics.

The aims of the task

- to teach the communication techniques needed to describe the overall form, parts and assembly of a product
- to develop an understanding of imagery used in promotion
- to enable students to develop high-quality making skills needed for a robust product
- to develop skills in simple decoration techniques.

Values

technical
Students should consider different kite designs and compare them for suitability for the task.

economic
Students should consider the value and purpose of promotional products.

aesthetic
Students should consider different cultural influences on the design and decoration of kites.

moral
Students should consider the use of a community event for commercial purposes.

social
Students should consider the role of community events such as a kite bonanza.

environmental
Students should consider the role of renewable materials in their designs.

Nature of the product

from exploration
The students should produce:
- an analysis of boxed cakes available
- a report on types of kite
- a preliminary specification of a new product
- a short report on the possibilities of converting cakes into kites.

for the production and promotion
The students should produce:
- a selection of product ideas which are evaluated against the product specification
- a detailed specification for the final product including materials, equipment, cost involved, production schedule and trial report
- a collection of images that could be used to advertise the kite bonanza on a poster.

possible products
- humming pie kite
- angel cake kite
- muffin marvel
- fairy flyer
- stunning sandwich cake
- cherry charmer
- baklava blower.

Technical knowledge and understanding

- knowledge and understanding of the range of techniques for decorating kites
- knowledge and understanding of the range of techniques for constructing kites
- knowledge of different kite designs.

Specialist tools, materials and equipment

- samples of commercial kites
- books of kites
- fabrics suitable for kites – tyvek, ripstop nylon, kite paper
- suitable adhesives
- specialist kite fixings and fittings.

Cross-curricular links

maths
- accurate measurement and scaling in developing designs from existing patterns.

science
- investigation in the factors affecting performance with a view to optimizing performance.

art
- simplification of images through observational drawing to give icons for decoration.

IT
- use of CAD/CAM to produce stencils for screen printing; use of DTP software to produce promotional material for the event.

economic and industrial understanding
- discussion of the costs and benefits of one-off advertising through events.

English
- writing copy for the promotional material.

Useful Resource Tasks

To develop an understanding of imagery used in promotion:
- CRT 1 *Mood boards and theme boards.*

To teach the communication techniques needed to describe the overall form, parts and assembly of a product:
- CRT 4 *Capturing fabric on paper*
- CRT 6 *Communicating to the maker.*

To enable students to develop high-quality making skills needed for a robust product:
- LIRT 4 *Kites and screen printing.*

To develop skills in simple decoration techniques:
- DRT 2 *Batik snowflakes.*

Useful Case Studies

To develop an understanding of imagery used in promotion:
'Corporate clothing' (*Student's Book*, page 48).

Design brief

To design and make a kite suitable to be flown as part of a promotion of confectionery.

Specification

What the product should do:
- fly well
- promote a product.

What the product should look like:
- be fun and intriguing (What's that supposed to be? Is that a flying éclair?).

Other features:
- fly in a variety of wind conditions
- be relatively easy to repair in event of crash landings.

Possible associated activities

- trial of commercial kites and report on their application to this task
- research into existing kite designs including those from other cultures
- brainstorm of cakes into kites.

Design sketches

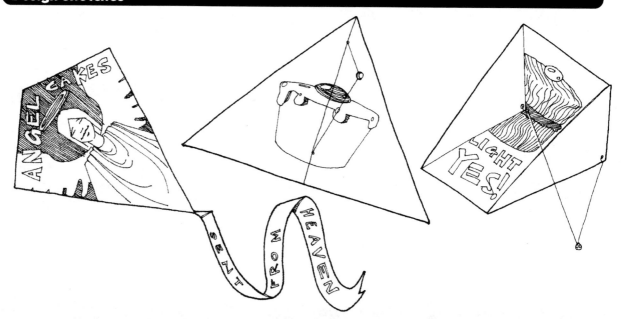

Information for making

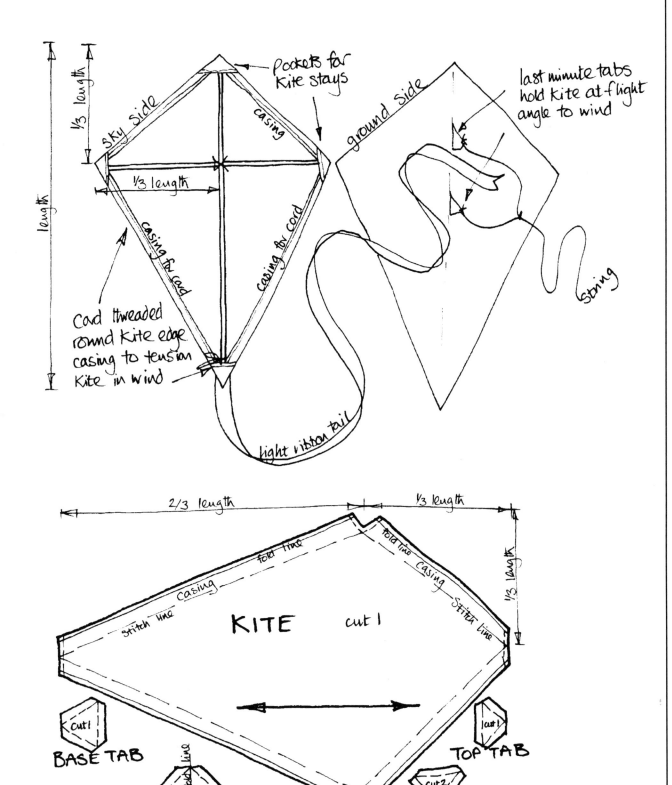

How will you check the kite will fly?

How can you keep the weight down to aid lift?

Resources
- light cane stays
- cord for casing
- ribbon for tail
- kite string

8 Clean cuisine

A Capability Task for textiles
Line of interest – protection

The task

To design and make to prototype stage an innovative range of protective clothing for the food industry – with emphasis on food handling in retail outlets.

Task setting

Although most people use supermarkets where they simply take food from the shelves, there is a growing emphasis on 'in-house personal service' areas in many large stores. Food Fare Inc. is one such store – it has specialist areas for fish, bread and cakes, meats and cheese.

The assistants are trained to serve and help select items for customers. Because they are handling food, the assistants must wear protective clothing, including a hat to contain their hair. Food Fare want the assistants to look right and feel happy in their uniform.

The aims of the task

- to enable students to investigate and analyse existing solutions (range of protective wear)
- to enable students to consider designing for a wide range of people (i.e. food assistants)
- to enable students to consider new developments in textile technology and their use (e.g. non-woven fabric)
- to enable students to present their design ideas with flair.

Values

technical
Students should consider the hygiene and comfort specifications of textiles.

economic
Students should consider the cost of disposable versus washable garments.

aesthetic
Students should consider the developments in protective clothing both historically and technologically.

moral
Students should consider if an encouragement to return to personal service in shops is desirable in modern society.

social
Students should consider the importance of acceptability and comfort in designing protective items.

environmental
Students should consider the materials and processes used in terms of their environmental impact (see economic).

Nature of the product

from exploration
The students should produce:
- a report on the range of protective clothing observed in local shops, with special emphasis on food handlers
- a report on the range of materials used in protective clothing. This could be based on a trade catalogue, specialist shop or direct observation
- a report on styles acceptable to the widest range of people. Head covering, trousers and shoes should be covered first.

for the production and promotion
The students should produce:
- a series of product ideas which are evaluated against the product specification
- a detailed specification for a final idea including materials, styles and care guidance
- a report on 'washable v. disposable' setting out the pros and cons
- a mood board which shows the product idea, including colour swatches
- a presentation sheet of the range for different sized/shaped/aged assistants.

possible products
- a prototype uniform to be tested for use. This may include:
  - cap
  - net
  - hat
  - waistcoat cum apron
  - trousers
  - wrap-around coverall
  - clogs
- a simple model of the food outlet, showing how the protective clothing complements/enhances the Food Fare Inc. corporate image.

Technical knowledge and understanding

- knowledge of material testing:
  - hygiene, comfort, durability, washability.
- knowledge of environmental health regulations
- knowledge and understanding of anthropometrics
- knowledge of fastening and trimmings for hygiene
- knowledge of sterilization techniques.

Specialist tools, materials and equipment

- range of textiles used in protective clothing
- range of non-woven fabrics
- 'popper' kit.

Cross-curricular links

maths
- 3D measurements, calculating 'best fit' from average.

science
- growth of bacteria on textiles.

art
- observational drawing to support fashion drawing.

IT
- use of CAD to explore colourways.

economic and industrial understanding
- the cost/benefits of disposable versus washable garments in the workplace; a look at the consequence of 'dirty practice' – any local environmental health official.

history
- the changing style of protective clothing – rubber aprons to plastic pinnies.

Useful Resource Tasks

To enable students to investigate and analyse existing solutions (range of protective wear):
- SRT 5 *Attribute analysis*.

To enable students to consider designing for a wide range of people (i.e. food assistants):
- SRT 2 *Questionnaires*.

To enable students to consider new developments in textile technologies and their use (e.g. non-woven fabric):
- FCRT 3 *Investigating the structure of fabrics*.

To enable students to present their design ideas with flair:
- CRT 3 *Fashion drawing*.

Useful Case Studies

To enable students to investigate and analyse existing solutions (range of protective wear):
'Corporate clothing' (*Student's Book*, page 48).

Design brief

To design and make a protective clothing collection that is suitable for wear in the food retail industry. It must be unisex in appeal and flexible in terms of size and shape. There should be presentation sheets of how the collection would be seen in the store. A fashion show for Food Fare Inc. should also be planned.

Specification

What the product should do:
- be hygienic
- cover all areas of risk
- be comfortable.

What the product should look like:
- be unisex
- be clean
- be innovative
- be attractive to both wearer and customer.

Other features:
- be washable/disposable.

Possible associated activities

- visit to food factory/shop to observe clothing
- use specialist catalogues to build up background information
- relate the protection clothing more to fashion than function, as in 'Funky Food Gear'.

Design sketches

Information for making

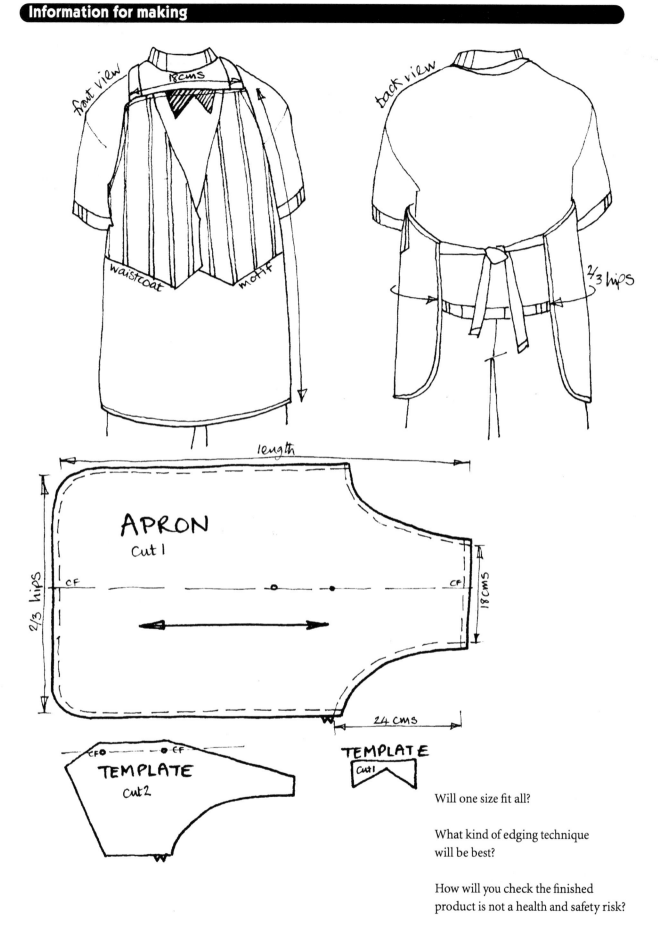

Will one size fit all?

What kind of edging technique will be best?

How will you check the finished product is not a health and safety risk?

Resources
- tape for ties and neck band

9 Travel safe

A Capability Task for textiles
Line of interest – protection

The task
To design and make a range of innovative textile products that both protect and promote safety in beginner cyclists.

Task setting
Thousands of children do their Cycling Proficiency certificates every year. They are normally aged between 10 and 11 years. Part of the training is the wearing of a protective helmet and reflective stripes on clothing. To market the idea of all-round safety, the Cycling Proficiency Scheme wants to develop a safety clothing identity. They would like ideas for a range of products that keep you safe on your bike while being attractive enough to attract attention and thus promote safety.

The aims of the task
- to enable students to design for a particular age group
- to teach the communication techniques needed to describe the parts, action and assembly of a product
- to enable students to select materials using a wide range of criteria and develop high-quality making skills
- to enable students to consider designing and making for manufacture when reviewing the feasibility of their product.

Values

technical
Students should consider the impact and importance of colour as part of safety on the road, and consider the durability of textiles for outdoor wear.

economic
Student should consider the added cost of safety to cycling for children and how marketing affects the sales of such products.

aesthetic
Students should consider how the image of safety wear can be enhanced and made desirable. How are helmets customized?

moral
Students should consider whether children should be encouraged to cycle on today's roads. Are a cycling proficiency certificate and 'travel safe' clothes enough?

social
Students should consider the influence of peer pressure on choices of safety wear. Is it cool to be safe?

environmental
Students should consider the environmental impact of cycling as opposed to other forms of transport, e.g. car, bus.

Nature of the product

from exploration
The students should produce:
- a report about current safety wear for cyclists
- a report on best colours, reflectors and textiles currently on the market which then develops ideas for visibility, durability and comfort
- preliminary sketches of current wear on bikes, drawn from observations (one hour watching and photographing the local main road)
- an analysis of a 'padded protector', e.g. skateboard knee pads, in order to inform own ideas
- a report on cycling accidents in the previous year showing causes and results
- a short case study on cycling helmets.

for the production and promotion
The students should produce:
- a selection of textile product ideas that are evaluated against the product specification
- a detailed specification of the final range of products which includes cost, materials, method of production and production schedule
- a breakdown of possible areas/types of protection needed
- to support the Cycling Proficiency Scheme, a life-size cut-out unisex figure that the Cycling Proficiency teacher can use as a demonstration.

possible products
As part of the range, products may include:
- visible 'bibs'
- fun exterior belts and braces
- elbow reflectors
- knee pads
- hand flashes
- helmet stretch nets
- jacket patches.

Technical knowledge and understanding
- knowledge of the properties and qualities of fabrics suitable for protective/visible clothing accessories
- knowledge of decorative techniques suitable for achieving visibility.

Specialist tools, materials and equipment
- range of protective clothing items
- seam ripper – to explore above
- cycling proficiency information
- ROSPA information pack
- test bike to ride.

Cross-curricular links

maths
- considering size limits for universal fit items.

science
- developing investigations to explore visibility in different lighting conditions.

art
- analysis of visual styles associated with products intended for 10/11-year-old children.

IT
- use of DTP software to produce an extra section for Cycling Proficiency Scheme.

economic and industrial understanding
- exploring the 'cost' of accidents in terms of prevention and remedial action.

music
- writing a jingle that could be part of a radio cycle safety campaign that coincides with a Cycling Proficiency Scheme.

English
- writing an extra section for the Cycling Proficiency Pack to encourage 'travel safety'.

Useful Resource Tasks

To enable students to design for a particular age group:
- SRT 1 *Identifying needs and likes.*

To teach the communication techniques needed to describe the parts, action and assembly of a product:
- CRT 4 *How to capture fabric on paper*
- CRT 6 *Communicating to the maker.*

To enable students to select materials using a wide range of criteria and develop high-quality making skills:
- SRT 4 *Brainstorming*
- LIRT 5 *Protection – quilted skating mitts.*

Useful Case Studies

'Protective clothing' (*Student's Book*, page 58).

To enable students to consider designing and making for manufacture when reviewing the feasibility of their product:
'Clothing manufacture' (*Student's Book*, page 70).

Design brief

To design and make a range of safety accessories that support a Cycling Proficiency Scheme for 10 year olds.

Specification

What the product should do:
- be acceptable wear for target group
- make cycling safer by making wearer more visible.

What the product should look like:
- be innovative, stylish, acceptable to young people.

Other features:
- be in keeping with Cycling Proficiency Scheme.

Possible associated activities

- visit primary school doing Cycling Proficiency Scheme
- research solutions through history of cyclists and safety
- interview police safety officer to get opinions.

Design sketches

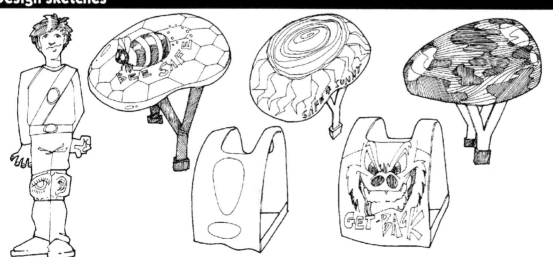

Information for making

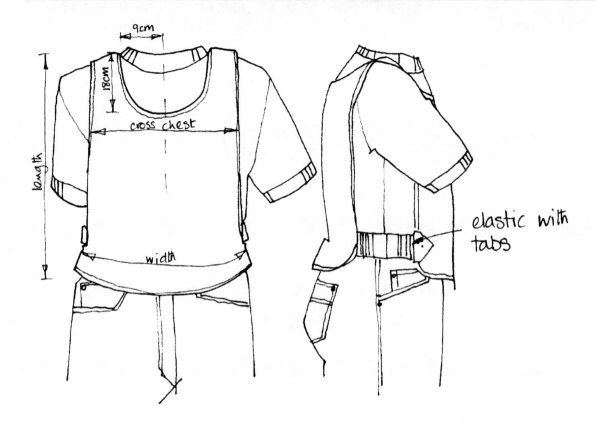

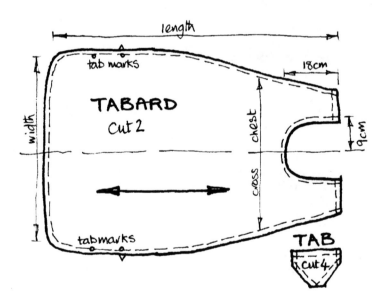

Will one size fit all?

Should the front and back be the same?

How will you test the safety features of the tabard?

What alternative methods of fastening are possible?

Resources
- binding for edges
- fastening for tabs
- wide elastic for side straps

Happy cotton 10

A Capability Task for textiles
Line of interest – street style

The task

To design and make to prototype stage a range of screen printed T-shirts that act as an environmental nudge, plus a display that illustrates eco-cotton production.

Task setting

There is a lot of information about the damage we are all doing to the environment. But there is also a good deal of misinformation. T-S-T-R-S – To Set The Record Straight – is an environmental consultancy that helps companies improve their public image. A major cotton producer, Happy Cotton Inc., wants to promote its new range of eco-cotton products. T-S-T-R-S are consulted as to how the public can be alerted to the change in practice in the cotton industry – no harmful bleaches, processes or productions. T-S-T-R-S come up with the idea of a T-shirt campaign.

The aims of the task

- to enable students to explore consumer response to issues
- to enable students to present complex information in an accessible way
- to enable students to acquire skills in screen printing and transfer printing
- to enable students to consider fabric production.

Values

technical
Students should consider the processes involved in the production of cotton and annotate possible danger spots for the environment.

economic
Students should investigate the cost implications of eco-friendly production methods.

aesthetic
Students should consider what looks effective as a placement print on a T-shirt, and consider what sort of display tells a textile story well.

moral
Students should consider the argument that we are stewards of the world and have an obligation to protect it for future inhabitants.

social
Students should consider the growth of the wearing of T-shirts as a social phenomenon. Does anyone not own a T-shirt?

environmental
Students should consider how the public can determine whether any so-called environmentally produced item really is so.

Nature of the product

from exploration
The students should produce:
- a report on slogans and effective visuals generally, then consider them on T-shirts
- exploration of simple screen printing techniques
- a range of messages, sentences, images
- a preliminary specification for the new product line that underlines the message, and the eco-inks and techniques used
- a display to show actual samples of cotton at various stages of production
- a T-shirt printed with a placement print that is at least A4 sized
- a short case study on Katherine Hamnett's sloganized T-shirts.

for the production and promotion
The students should produce:
- a selection of ideas that are evaluated against the product specification
- a detailed specification for the final product that focuses on the environmental messages and impact
- a collection of images that could be used as an advertisement on a billboard or in a magazine.

possible products
- T-shirts with printed images/slogans such as:
  - 'Happy Cotton Bud' ©
  - 'Cotton-u-like'
  - 'Cotton on – it's OK'
  - 'Cool Cotton – does no harm'
- a zigzag storyboard
- an image board for T-shirts as part of a display.

Technical knowledge and understanding

- knowledge of how cotton is produced
- knowledge of how T-shirts are printed.

Specialist tools, materials and equipment

- range of ready-made T-shirts
- catalogues of T-shirts
- eco-friendly inks and dyes
- photocopier for pattern development.

Cross-curricular links

maths
- cost implication ratios of eco-friendly inks versus normal commercial products for a variety of run lengths.

science
- investigating the effects of bleaching through experiments and second-hand data leading to a short case study of this.

art
- analysis of visual form to consider effective lettering.

IT
- use of CAD/CAM to produce screens for printing; use of DTP software for developing display material.

economic and industrial understanding
- the environment as the most recent marketing tool.

Useful Resource Tasks

To enable students to explore consumer response to issues:
- SRT 1 *Identifying needs and likes*
- SRT 2 *Questionnaires.*

To enable students to present complex ideas in an accessible way:
- CRT 1 *Mood boards and theme boards*
- CRT 2 *Presenting data.*

To enable students to acquire skills in screen printing and transfer printing:
- LIRT 4 *Kites and screen printing*
- LIRT 6 *Street style T-shirt and baseball cap decoration.*

Useful Case Studies

To enable students to consider fabric production:
'Saidpur women textile group Bangladesh' (*Student's Book*, page 62).

Design brief

To design and make a display that illustrates the production of eco-friendly cotton and a cotton product that carries a message to promote the new cotton.

Specification

the display
What the product should do:
- illustrate the story of eco-cotton.

What the product should look like:
- be striking
- be engaging.

Other features:
- be accessible to a wide audience
- be easy to put up and take down.

the T-shirt
What the product should do:
- show a strong message
- raise awareness of environmental issues.

What the product should look like:
- be a street style T-shirt
- be striking and engaging (controversial?)

Other features:
- should form part of a series
- image should have long life despite wear and care.

Possible associated activities

- visit local stores to analyse T-shirts with slogans
- investigate products produced under environmental name
- survey students' attitudes in school
- brainstorm slogans that really work.

Design sketches

10 Happy cotton

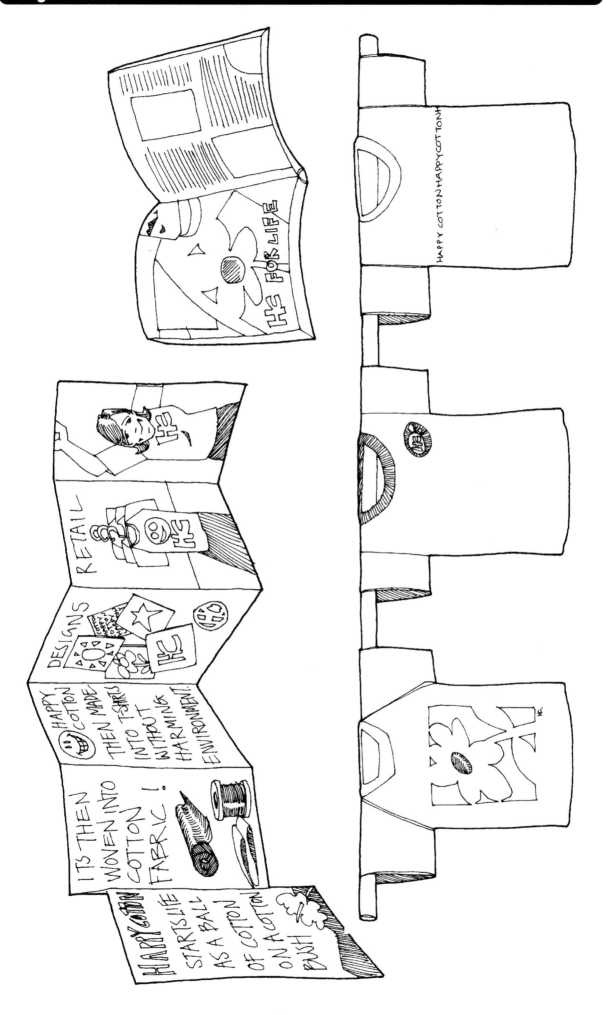

Information for making

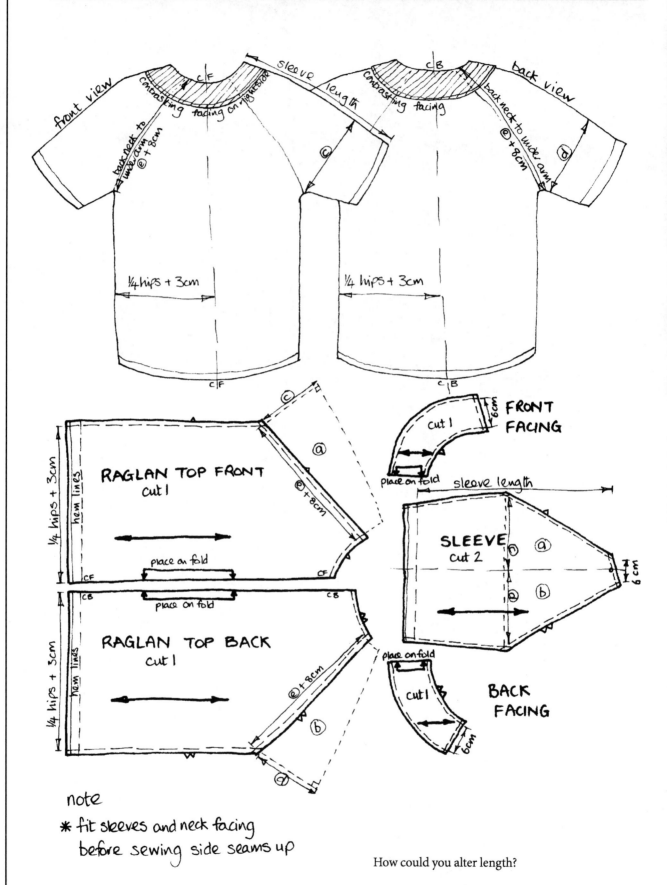

note
* fit sleeves and neck facing before sewing side seams up

How could you alter length?

What hemming technique would be best?

Rap wrap 11

A Capability Task for textiles
Line of interest – street style

The task
To design and make a dressing gown that reflects current street style.

Task setting
American teenagers in the 1950s started a fashion for outdoor jackets with slogans, college names and emblems on them. These short zipped jackets were made from a variety of materials including leather. Rap Wear Ltd is a clothing manufacturer with its eye firmly on the young market. It has decided to develop a range of themed wrap-around dressing gowns, for men and women, based on the jackets of the 1950s. Obviously you would not want a leather kimono but the company would like its rap wraps to be as current as possible. What would be appropriate symbols, words or applied decorations for today? Could these wraps be sold for after-sports wear?

The aims of the task
- to enable students to design from a theme
- to enable students to present their design ideas with flair
- to teach the communication techniques needed to describe the overall form, parts and assembly of a product
- to enable students to develop skills in appliqué and embroidery.

Values

technical
Students should consider issues of wear, comfort and washability.

economic
Students should consider issues of 'added value' with craft-based products.

aesthetic
Students should consider how today's decoration can reflect the feel of the times, in much the way that the American college jackets did in the 1950s.

moral
Students should consider the pay and conditions of many workers who add value through craft-based activities.

social
Students should consider style as reflected in street style fashions.

environmental
Students should consider how recycled materials might be used in their products.

Nature of the product

from exploration
The students should produce:
- a report on decorated jackets
- a comparison of different methods and techniques of applying decoration to textile products
- simple ideas for the dressing gown shape
- a collection of present-day images and symbols
- a preliminary specification of a new product, e.g. a 'themed' wrap, based on football in the 90s
- a short report on existing products, looking at the range, price, appeal and any applied decoration.

for the production and promotion
The students should produce:
- a selection of textile ideas which are evaluated against the specification, including materials, equipment, cost, production schedule, time taken
- a collection of images that could be used as an advertisement on a billboard or in a magazine.

possible products
- animal wrap
- wild wrap
- sports gown
- dressing-up gown
- champion wrap

all with applied decorative detail to illustrate themes.

Technical knowledge and understanding
- knowledge and understanding of how dressing gowns are constructed
- knowledge and understanding of appliqué and embroidery.

Specialist tools, materials and equipment
- range of textiles including wadding for analysis and trial
- publications with examples of 1950s' jackets.

Cross-curricular links

maths
- measurement in pattern cutting; ratio in considering scale of decoration to garments.

science
- investigation of thermal and absorbency properties of fabrics.

art
- analysing images of today and yesterday to find their key elements.

IT
- use of CAD/CAM to produce pattern template for appliqué; use of CAD/CAM to produce embroidery-based decoration.

economic and industrial understanding
- the role of craft work in high-value goods.

Useful Resource Tasks

To enable students to design from a theme:
- CRT 1 *Mood boards and theme boards*.

To enable students to present their design ideas with flair:
- CRT 3 *Fashion drawing*.

To teach the communication techniques needed to describe the overall form, parts and assembly of a product:
- CRT 6 *Communicating to the maker*.

To enable students to develop skills in appliqué and embroidery:
- LIRT 3 *Interiors – a wall hanging for a child's bedroom*.

Useful Case Studies

To enable students to design from a theme:
'Design in the High Street' (*Student's Book*, page 50),
'New fashion textiles' (*Student's Book*, page 53).

Design brief

To design and make a modern dressing gown that reflects the street style of today in a similar way to American jackets in the 1950s.

Specification

What the product should do:
- serve as a dressing gown.

What the product should look like:
- appeal to young people, i.e. funky yet wearable; dangerous yet comfortable.

Other features:
- include fabric appliqué and embroidery techniques.

Possible associated activities

- visit museum to observe fashions and street styles of other times
- comment on today's street styles
- produce small samples of applied decoration as investigations
- produce image board, half to reflect style of 1950s half to reflect today
- produce grid sheet of drawings of simple dressing gowns hanging on poles poking through arms, with ideas on the back
- produce toiles, i.e. calico rough dressing gown to pin ideas on back and thus get idea of dimensions.

Design sketches

Information for making

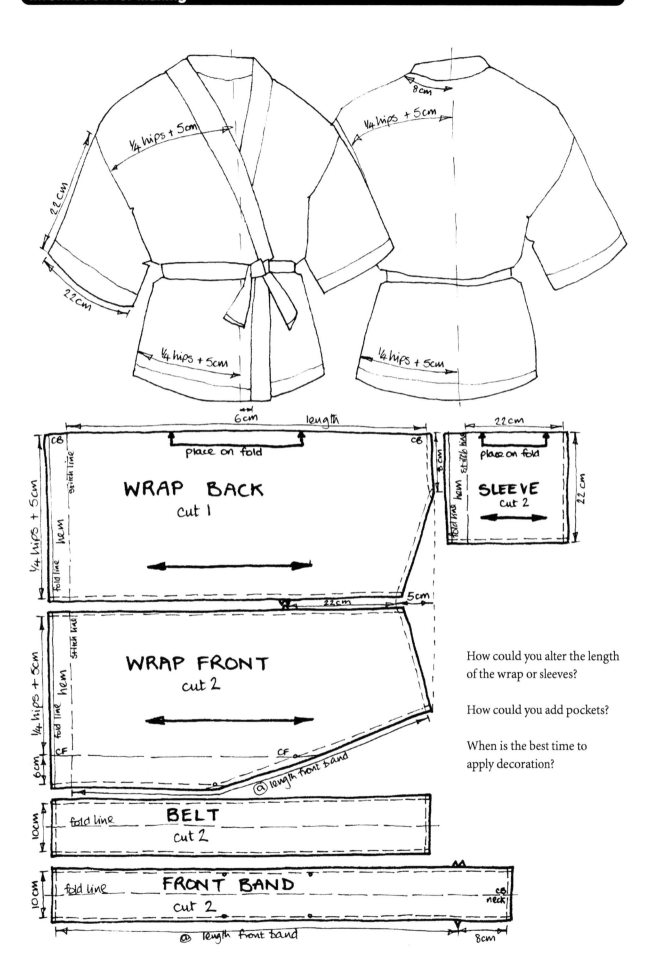

How could you alter the length of the wrap or sleeves?

How could you add pockets?

When is the best time to apply decoration?

12 Snuggly buggly

A Capability Task for textiles
Line of interest – tents

The task
To design and make an indoor tent as a play space for young children.

Task setting
Young children love to create their own small worlds by playing in 'home corners', tents or other play spaces. Most modern homes are not large enough to accommodate a permanent indoor play structure for them, so a major tent manufacturer, Groundsheets Ltd, wants ideas for simple, colourful indoor 'tents' that can be erected or put away quickly and that would serve as private play spaces for young children. Safety and stability are prime considerations. Groundsheets Ltd also needs to think how and where these small persons' tents could be sold.

The aims of the task
- to enable students to design for a particular age group
- to enable students to consider factors such as stability and collapsibility
- to teach the communication techniques needed to describe the parts, action and assembly of a product
- to enable students to select materials using a wide range of criteria and develop high-quality making skills.

Values

technical
Students should consider how technical expertise will contribute to the safety aspects of their design.

economic
Students should consider the market for children's products.

aesthetic
Students should consider what appeals to young children in terms of shape, colour and texture.

moral
Students should consider the worth of such a product compared to the DIY alternative of a blanket and a broom stick.

social
Students should consider the value of play afforded by small play spaces for young children.

environmental
Students should consider the source and means of production of the materials they choose.

Nature of the product

from exploration
The students should produce:
- a report on the use of small play spaces by young children
- a report on self-supporting tents commercially available
- a report on colours, shapes, and themes to appeal to the age range of the children
- several prototype geometric shapes should be explored
- a preliminary specification for a new product
- a one-kid tent that can stand unsupported and packs away flat
- a short case study of a recent new tent based on visits to camping shops.

for the production and promotion
The students should produce:
- a selection of product ideas which are evaluated against the product specification
- a detailed specification for the final product including materials, equipment, cost involved and production schedule, plus market testing
- an information sheet using pictures that details how to erect and dismantle the tent.

possible products
- building-block bungalows
- tepees for tots
- liquorice allsorts houses
- sweet dreams

all constructed from strong fabric, stiffened with 'ribs'.

Technical knowledge and understanding
- knowledge and understanding of safety considerations of products for children
- knowledge and understanding of fabric-based structural forms.

Specialist tools, materials and equipment
- range of stiffeners
- catalogues of camping equipment
- catalogues of play equipment
- video of children at play in a nursery.

Cross-curricular links

maths
- measurement of volume of geometric shapes; nets for modelling ideas.

science
- understanding of the forces in a simple structure (tension and compression) and how textiles will respond.

art
- ways of simplifying complex forms into elements that become suitable for designing and making, e.g. a caterpillar tent.

IT
- use of CAD/CAM to produce innovative embroidery-based decoration.

economic and industrial understanding
- ways of simplifying the design to make it easier and less costly to manufacture without loss of customer appeal should be discussed.

Useful Resource Tasks

To enable students to design for a particular age group:
- SRT 1 *Identifying needs and likes.*

To teach the communication techniques needed to describe the parts, action and assembly of a product:
- CRT 4 *How to capture fabric on paper*
- CRT 6 *Communicating to the maker.*

To enable students to select materials using a wide range of criteria and develop high-quality making skills:
- SRT 5 *Attribute analysis*
- SRT 4 *Brainstorming*
- LIRT 7 *Tents – investigating seams, reinforcements and loops.*

Useful Case Studies

To enable students to consider factors such as stability and collapsibility:
'A tent for your home' (*Student's Book*, page 57).

Design brief

To design and make an indoor tent-like structure that is suitable as an easily erected and collapsed play space for young children.

Specification

What the product should do:
- provide a private play space.

What the product should look like:
- be attractive to young children
- be based on a recognizable theme.

Other features:
- be small enough to be used indoors
- be safe, i.e. stable, rigid, fireproof
- be collapsible.

Possible associated activities

- visit to a nursery school
- visit to a camping shop
- talk from teacher/camping specialist
- research into ways of stiffening fabric
- investigation of textile-based shapes for the structures through small model.

Design sketches

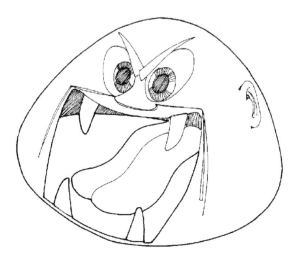

Information for making

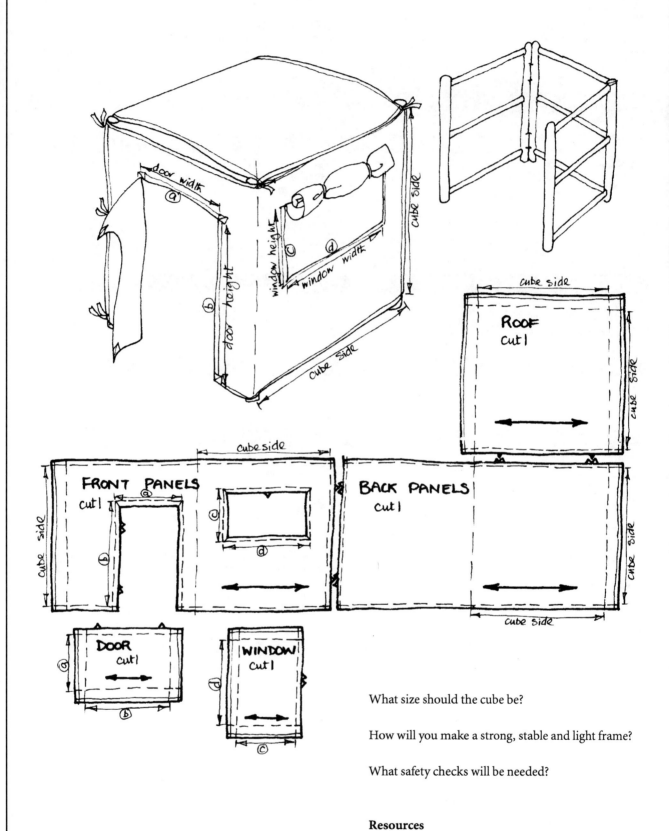

What size should the cube be?

How will you make a strong, stable and light frame?

What safety checks will be needed?

Resources
- material for frame (bars, hinges)
- fastening for door

A cast of thousands — 13

A Capability Task for textiles
Line of interest – the theatre

The task

To design and make a flexible garment that could be adapted for use in several school productions.

Task setting

Most schools put on productions, whether it is drama or dance. Nothing looks worse than scrappy costumes for the crowd or group scenes. Of course it is very costly to make up to 100 costumes. A leading pattern company – Fit-U – have an idea to produce a basic garment that could be adapted for a range of school productions. They have identified the following as examples.

- children in *Oliver!* (singing)
- crowds at a football match (chanting)
- a living wood (dance/drama).

They need the garment prototyped and visual presentations of how one garment could be adapted for the three roles above.

The aims of the task

- to enable students to present their design ideas with flair
- to teach the communication techniques needed to describe the parts, action and assembly of a product
- to enable students to consider costs and present costing information in an attractive manner
- to enable students to cut simple patterns and develop high-quality making skills.

Values

technical
Students should consider the use of adjustability in providing standard costumes that fit a variation in size.

economic
Students should consider the cost implications of ten costumes, used in the three productions. How much per unit?

aesthetic
Students should consider how dramatic effects can be achieved.

moral
Students should consider the arguments for and against censorship in the theatre.

social
Students should consider the importance of including 'all' in school productions, not just the stars.

environmental
Students should consider the role of recycled textiles in their products.

Nature of the product

from exploration
The students should produce:
- a collection of ideas for the three productions
- suggestions for simple-shaped garments
- a list of possible accessories to use in the different productions
- a tacked prototype(s) of the garment(s)
- a preliminary specification for four products:
  - basic garment
  - accessory for Oliver
  - accessory for crowd scene
  - accessory for wild wood
- a short case study from a personal standpoint of costumes used in a recent TV production.

for the production and promotion
The students should produce:
- a selection of ideas which are evaluated against the product specification
- a detailed specification for the final product which includes fabric used, techniques, paper pattern, cost, time production schedule
- a collection of images that could be used in the production programme.

possible products
- T-shaped black garment
- waistcoat
- tabard
- cloak/wrap
- range of accessories to convert simple garment to costume for each of the productions.

Technical knowledge and understanding

- knowledge of simple pattern shapes
- knowledge of properties and qualities of textiles – durability, comfort, colour and texture
- knowledge of stage lighting and its effect on costume.

Specialist tools, materials and equipment

- figure form for fitting
- access to theatrical/costume magazines or equivalent CD-ROM.

Cross-curricular links

maths
- accurate measurement to ensure best fit for most people; averages and how they apply to costume; volume of storage needed for ten costumes.

science
- exploration of washability and durability of range of fabrics; investigation of effect of stage lighting on costume appearance.

art
- exploration of other people's interpretation of the costumes for the productions.

IT
- use of spreadsheet for investigating costs of mounting productions.

economic and industrial understanding
- exploration of the finances of a school production.

drama
- writing a short extract from each production; experiment in groups.

Useful Resource Tasks

To enable students to present their design ideas with flair:
- CRT 1 *Mood boards and theme boards*
- CRT 3 *Fashion drawing*.

To teach the communication techniques needed to describe the parts, action and assembly of a product:
- CRT 6 *Communicating to the maker*.

To enable students to consider costs and present costing information in an attractive manner:
- CRT 2 *Presenting data*.

To enable students to cut simple patterns and develop high-quality making skills:
- LIRT 8 *The theatre – Costumes for a dance routine*.

Useful Case Studies

'Design in the High Street' (*Student's Book*, page 50).

Design brief

To design and make an adaptable garment to be used for a range of school productions, and three accessories suitable for different productions.

Specification

What the product(s) should do:
- provide a basic garment that can be adapted for different productions
- provide accessories that are suitable for the adaptations.

What the product should look like:
- be dramatic and striking
- be appropriate to the productions.

Other features:
- be adaptable for a range of sizes
- be washable and durable
- be simple and easy to get on and off
- be light and comfortable
- be low cost.

Possible associated activities

- visit to theatre or theatre wardrobe department to see professional approaches
- watch film/video where groups of people are costumed – make notes of basic shapes and structures
- research into costume for the theatre, particularly for school productions if possible
- image boards for each production showing 'big' ideas, e.g. *Oliver!* – rags and tatters; football – scarves and mouths; wild wood – movement and leaves.

Design sketches

13 A cast of thousands

Information for making

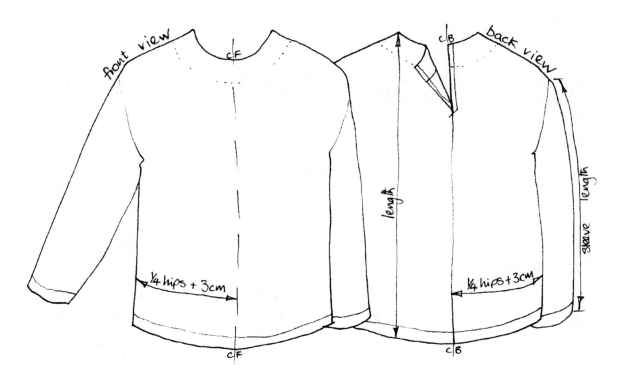

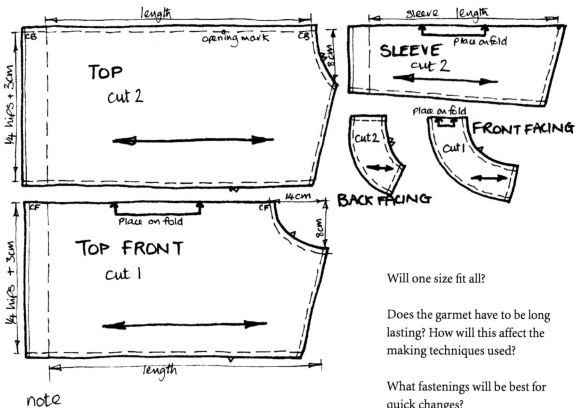

note

∗ to make a longer version, it will be necessary to flair the side seam out from the underarm point.

Will one size fit all?

Does the garmet have to be long lasting? How will this affect the making techniques used?

What fastenings will be best for quick changes?

Resources
- fastening

Audition kit bag

14

A Capability Task for textiles
Line of interest – the theatre

The task

To design and make a range of textile products that can be used as quick-change items for an audition for TV. Each item must help set the scene for the actor/actress. They should be small enough to be stowed in an 'audition kit bag', which should form part of the task.

Task setting

Going to auditions is part of what every actor/actress has to do. Often they know the part they are auditioning for but sometimes they are just asked to 'show us what you can do'. A performing arts school wants to train its students to be as flexible as possible for these auditions so has come up with the idea of an audition kit bag. The school wants all the items to be textile based so that they can be worn and carried easily.

The aims of the task

- to enable students to design for a particular client
- to enable students to present their design ideas with flair
- to teach the communication techniques needed to describe the parts, action and assembly of a product
- to enable students to cut simple patterns and develop high-quality making skills.

Values

technical
Students should consider the need for ease of care in the materials chosen for the props.

economic
Students should consider the actual cost of this kit and compare it to the cost if bought separately and assembled, and consider other markets for this product.

aesthetic
Students should consider how different decorative finishes to fabrics achieve dramatic effects.

moral
Students should consider the arguments for and against censorship in the theatre.

social
Students should consider the range of characters/situations that could give contrast socially.

environmental
Students should consider the role of recycled textiles in their products.

Nature of the product

from exploration
The students should produce:
- a description of three possible characters from literature and what they would say
- sketches of key items of dress that suggest a character
- lists of possible characters from plays
- a preliminary specification, e.g. an audition shoe-bag kit; bow tie, hat and waistcoat.

for the production and promotion
The students should produce:
- a booklet that describes the contents, the characters and gives examples of their lines
- a short case study of three TV characters whose clothing is significant
- a selection of textile prototypes which are evaluated against the specification
- a detailed specification for the final kit that details materials, equipment, method of production, schedule, cost, etc.

possible products
- hat
- crown
- armour
- cloak
- mask
- bow tie
- scarf
- pinafore
- sash.

Technical knowledge and understanding

- knowledge of simple pattern shapes
- knowledge of properties and qualities of textiles – durability, comfort, colour and texture.

Specialist tools, materials and equipment

- access to a range of play manuscripts
- wide range of textiles that includes stockinet, muslin, calico, felt and netting
- wide range of decorating finishes and trimmings, e.g. sequins, lace
- fabric glues.

Audition kit bag 14

Cross-curricular links

maths
- measurement to ensure good and easy fit; calculations to keep costs low.

science
- exploration to find fabrics which are particularly easy to care for.

art
- analysis of costume to identify key visual elements to inform prop design.

IT
- use of DTP software to produce short playlets to accompany the audition kit bag.

economic and industrial understanding
- an investigation into the salaries of actors and actresses in different parts of the entertainment industry.

drama
- students should consider characterization and the importance of costume.

English
- written piece on 'My audition for *Brookside*'.

Useful Resource Tasks

To enable students to design for a particular client:
- SRT 1 *Identifying needs and likes.*

To enable students to present their design ideas with flair:
- CRT 1 *Mood boards and theme boards*
- CRT 3 *Fashion drawing.*

To teach the communication techniques needed to describe the parts, action and assembly of a product:
- CRT 6 *Communicating to the maker.*

To enable students to cut simple patterns and develop high-quality making skills:
- LIRT 8 *The theatre – Costumes for a dance routine.*

Useful Case Studies

'Design in the High Street' (*Student's Book*, page 50).

Design brief

To design and make an audition kit bag that contains three textile items that help bring a character to life.

Specification

What the product should do:
- provide a set of textile-based props to illustrate a character
- fit into a bag.

What the product should look like:
- be in keeping with the character to be portrayed
- be inherently attractive.

Other features:
- be easy to use
- be easy to care for.

Possible associated activities

- watch TV to research and identify significant pieces of costume
- investigate a range of children's books, e.g. what could help portray *Thomas the Tank Engine*?
- an actor/actress to visit the school and talk about auditioning for roles
- a visit to a costume hire shop
- a visit to an infant school to observe favourite dressing-up items in textiles.

© The Nuffield Foundation, 1996

Design sketches

14 Audition kit bag

Information for making

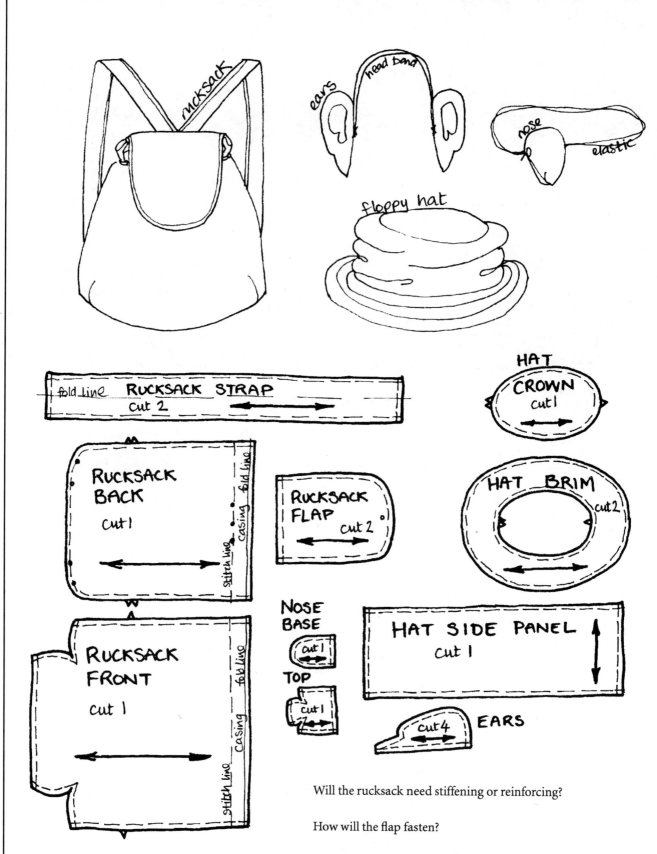

Will the rucksack need stiffening or reinforcing?

How will the flap fasten?

How will you check the length of the straps?

Resources
- fastening and cord for rucksack
- wadding for brim